Quest
for
Community

Quest
for
Community
Tomorrow's Parish Today

Dennis J.
Geaney, OSA

AVE MARIA PRESS   NOTRE DAME, INDIANA 46556

Acknowledgment

I wish to acknowledge William Droel's contribution to this book. From start to finish he critiqued my work with his sharp pencil. Without his encouragement it would not have been published.

Permission

Excerpts from THE JERUSALEM BIBLE, copyright © 1966 by Darton, Longman & Todd, Ltd. and Doubleday & Company, Inc. Used by permission of the publisher.

Library of Congress Catalog Card Number: 87-71612

International Standard Book Number: 0-87793-368-5

Manufactured in the United States of America

Contents

Introduction

The Catholic church, which has survived 20 centuries of being domesticated by cultures and governments, is today challenged, particularly in North America, by an individualism that runs counter to Christianity's communitarian roots.

David C. Leege, in *The Notre Dame Study of Catholic Parish Life*, writes:

> Social commentators identify the loss of a sense of community as a central problem of our times. Society has gotten complex and crowded. Work is often specialized, anonymous, and its products distant. Residential life is privatized, often far removed from work life or civic involvements. A deep chasm is said to separate private morality from public morality. In pursuit of excellence, acquisitions, or prominence, the individual becomes self-absorbed and narcissistic. Both public policy and consumer appeals make the individual the object of the "pursuit of happiness" or the "good." . . .

The Second Vatican Council called for the church not only to assert the primacy of God in Christ and the enduring need for the salvation of the individual, but also to infuse itself in the surrounding cultures. God works through human culture, sinful though it is; revelation is embedded in human symbols. When dominant cultural trends run in directions contrary to the enduring faith, the church focuses its sights on root causes in the culture. Confronting excessive individualism with Christian perspectives on community becomes a task especially for the local parish.[1]

In answer to this challenge, many church leaders see glimpses of communitarian gospel values in practice in the base community movement in other parts of the world. They are enamored with the freshness and vitality emerging from the small Christian communities in the barrios of Latin America, the villages of Africa and the farm communities of the Philippines.

However, any interest in the base community model taking root in the North American church must respect its cultural history. The gospel does not take flesh in theories, ideologies, or programs, but in people whose stories make them unique.

Since the Second Vatican Council, the Catholic church has come to see itself as a cloister for the disciples of Jesus — a place where people withdraw from secular pursuits to seek God in communion with other kindred spirits. With holiness as the universal call, monasteries or cloisters must be designed in the midst of the busyness of life. The parish has the possibility.

If community is perceived as face-to-face relationships in which people can bond in small groups to share their journey, the parish must be structured to provide nourishment for all. It must also provide an opportunity for small groups to emerge and form a life of their own while linked to the resources of the wider church. David Leege lends support to this notion when he writes:

> A parish or a congregation can be a "community of memory" — linking the stories of the past to the problems of the present and the visions of the future. Individuals in parishes are not isolated historically: they learn both the heroic deeds and dismal failings of their ancestors in the faith; they brush their contemporaries and may even come to share their joys and sorrows; and they are united in a vision of a future that both judges and gives hope for the present.[2]

This book addresses itself to parishes

and small communities that are seeking the reign of God in the myriad situations of daily life. I write about parishes across the country that are consciously trying to shift from a consumer to a community orientation, that seek to give owner-ship to their members and have deep convictions about the Jesus Story. Consumer parishes offer a myriad of services to individuals while commu-nity parishes focus on liturgies that are gather-ings of celebration, places where the Story is heard in a manner that touches people's lives, and where there is evident outreach to a wider community. It focuses on parishes that I believe effectively tell the Story.

My underlying assumptions in the book are:

1) The friendship model of two or three gathered in the name of Jesus is the basic model of Christianity.

2) The twos and threes must be gathered into networks which collectively give us the cath-olicity of church.

3) While the basic insight of the base com-munities of Latin America is the two and three gathered, its North American form will be shaped by our history and culture.

4) While each parish is unique, there are

types that are shaped by such factors as size, geography, income levels, race, ethnicity, and the personality of the pastor.

5) Any suggested programs or approaches must be adapted to fit the uniqueness of the parish.

6) An American spirituality is unfolding. American culture, with its strengths and weaknesses, will influence the spirituality of the parishes and their people. Hopefully our parishes will be a countercultural force in reshaping our values.

I begin each chapter with one or more parish profiles that focus on a particular facet of community. The chapter itself will not amplify all the issues raised in a particular narrative, but I hope that collectively, through narrative and text, a vision of Christian community stemming from parish life will be clear.

My interviews with parish members are impressionistic. I make no attempt to catch all the facets of parish life. The parishes are limited to ones with which I am familiar and could travel to, given the constraints of being committed to work as an associate pastor. Forty years of parish watching, however, assure me that these parishes represent examples of an American Catholic church that supports my view of an alive parish — that is, one that offers a forthright gospel challenge to its members and our culture, the type of parish that has a future.

My thesis is that the communitarian model of parish is the only model that can comfort and confront the individualistic, middle class, upward-bound Catholic.

This model must be strong in three facets of parish life: formation, worship and outreach. All of them must function well in reinforcing each other. Doing well in one or two of these areas is not enough. From the strength of this triad will come warmth and welcome and spiritual friendship that hopefully will express themselves in several intentional small groups within the parish.

Leege emphasizes the importance of rootedness for a parish as community. He writes:

> Rev. Philip Murnion argues that parish as community is not a product solely of friendliness but of feeling rootedness. The loss of community comes when common faith, common worship, and a common way of life are lacking. Recovery of community is assisted through a clear proclamation of faith and social ethics by the bishops. But even then a dialogue about faith and ethics must ensue in

the parish for that community to embrace it as *their* faith and *their* ethics. Often that dialogue takes the form of community actions that share joy, grief, or suffering. . . . To return to Murnion's metaphor, roots sink in soil and draw vitality from the nutrients around them.

Some of the nutrients are nurtured by pastors and church professionals who enable the laity to grow, to settle on common parish goals, to identify parish needs and develop community-run ministries toward those needs. Nutrients also come from liturgies that build community, that recognize the *community* as sacramental when it joins around the sacrament it celebrates, that encourage the peoples' participation in liturgical acts, and proclaim the relevance of scriptural and church teachings to both public and private morality.[3]

The communitarian parish is significantly different from the model operative as recently as 20 years ago. The sociologists of religion have been studying Catholic practices and attitudes for the past three decades, notably at the National Opinion Research Center. The Notre Dame Study of Catholic Parish Life has made a significant contribution to an understanding of how parish life is lived and perceived by parishioners.

What is needed now are stories that give flesh to the data.

I make no apology for this book being impressionistic and judgmental. The subtitle could easily be "In My Opinion."

Notes

1. David C. Leege, "The Parish as Community," *The Notre Dame Study of Catholic Parish Life* (No. 10, March, 1987), p. 1.

2. Ibid. pp. 1-2.

3. Ibid. p. 2.

Chapter One

The Quest for Community

One of my roles as a parish priest is liturgical greeter. At the weekend liturgies I go up and down the aisles before each Mass playing the jester or clown, warming up the people for a joyful celebration of the Eucharist.

I play with the children, ask elderly people about their lumbago or fallen arches — or more seriously, how they are managing the recent death of a spouse. The over-all goal is to pull people into a feeling of relatedness. I am trying to mount the barriers of an individualistic piety and get people out of their self-centeredness and into the Body of Christ. By smiles, laughter, and a few caring words, I try to bring people from their private commerce with God into a worshiping community. Until recently, American Catholics made the Eucharist a private devotion, like prayer at a shrine rather than fellowship at the table of the Lord. As Italian mothers created family warmth at table with their special spaghetti sauce, I am trying to build community out of the love and caring in the worshipers' hearts — ingredients that crave expression.

The Jesus Story needs to be heard by a community of fellow travelers, people struggling with the dream of Jesus calling them to an inner freedom. My welcoming posture sets the stage for the Story to be told and listened to by people who hopefully are becoming more committed to Jesus Christ as they deepen the bonds among themselves, as they assimilate the readings and homily.

Every Christian community needs to hear the Story over and over again through reading the scriptures aloud, through reflection and discussion in order to assess its implications for whatever situation the community faces. It shapes the community and becomes the wheel on which our lives turn. If the Story does not generate change in our personal, family and work lives and places, the community that hears it is simply a discussion group, not an apostolic center for bringing the Good News to the community.

Does the Story still have the power to give

hope to working parents, to couples in loveless marriages, to the Yuppies, to students concerned about SAT scores? Does it help to sort out our values as our culture forces us to choose from a variety of lifestyles?

In the eucharistic prayer the assembly members ritualize their oneness by eating the bread and drinking from the cup. This is the formula of theologian John Shea: "Gather the folks, tell the Story, and break the Bread."

"To Create a Community of Friends"

The chairperson of the Christian Service Committee of Blessed Sacrament parish in South Charleston, an industrial city in West Virginia, invited me to conduct a workshop or day of renewal based on my book, *The Prophetic Parish.* The idea came not from a staff member but from a volunteer, which gave me a clue that lay ownership was an important element in the organization of this parish.

On the way from the airport to the parish it was obvious that what had been a quiet Southern town of small businesses and farms had become an industrial center. In the past ten years several world-renowned chemical companies and some runaway Rust Belt plants had moved there, offering work to underemployed locals. But new industry can raise the anxiety level of a town. Workers and their families live with the threat of the operation being moved to yet another part of the world leaving heavy unemployment for the hourly workers and the need for technicians and executives to relocate. How do these people relate to a parish, to Sunday liturgy, to justice concerns? I may have something to offer but much more to learn, I thought, as I drove past a half mile of chemical plants.

The pastor, Father Jodi DeBais, was genuinely hospitable. My first question was "What is your basic goal as pastor?" He replied, "To create a community of friends." This was demonstrated that evening. The host committee and kindred people in other parishes held a dinner the day before the workshop so that they might have an opportunity to meet with me informally. Community building was in motion from the moment I arrived.

And there were more elements to come. At the Sunday liturgy a greeter with a name tag, "Helen Smith, Greeter" welcomed me and all arriving parishioners in the foyer. Inside the worship area were other greeters formally known as ushers. Before the pastor vested he stood in the midst of the people and asked visitors to identify themselves and meet the parishioners. He also made the announcements and other comments in an informal manner. After the liturgy no one hurried to the parking lot. The atmosphere was contagious. Parishioners not only prayed together but savored each other in small, friendly talk.

In our brief initial conversation the pastor hit me with a shocker. "I am glad we don't have a school. I hear other pastors talk about the parish school, finances, fund raisers and the like. I find it divisive." This is American Catholic church heresy. He is choosing hospitality and community over formal Catholic education.

Blessed Sacrament church was originally built as the top floor of the school building. When enrollment declined, the previous pastor closed the school, which angered some parishioners who subsequently left.

The pastor then built a modern worship center which opened into the former school allowing access to parish meeting rooms and religious education classrooms. It was clear from my visit that the present pastor was building on the vision of his predecessor in making worship central to Christian community.

The Christian Service Committee of Blessed Sacrament is a small group of people, mostly women, who initiate and support local caring projects. My agenda was to widen their horizons about care for the earth, water and sky, to proclaim a seemingly impossible peace in the face of the nuclear weapons race. Such a subject has enough appeal in any parish to fill a standard size phone booth. My goal was to take advantage of the climate of friendliness and offer a challenge spiced with humor and love that would keep them listening.

I did not work in a vacuum. Blessed Sacrament had a history to build on. Its Tithe Fund receives 7.5 percent of the general parish revenue. A Christian Service Committee recommends to the parish council how the Tithe Fund is allocated. It works like the United Way or the Campaign for Human Development with local groups making presentations to the committee.

Among recipients of money from the Tithe Fund are the local Covenant House for abused women, the Catholic Community Services, West Virginia Health Right, Inc., Bread for the World, Meals on Wheels, Manor Meal, and Heart and Hand House. Through the Tithe Fund parishioners are pulled into a wide variety of human services and they learn about the local agencies. In the process many enlist as volunteers. The parish is not setting itself up to respond to every need, but there seemed to be no end to the information given me by parishioners at the workshop. Amnesty International and prison ministry were explained by parishioners. In a largely Protestant town, Blessed Sacrament respects and works with the ecumenical, private and public agencies. The Last Judgment gospel (Matthew 25) is lived in this parish whose goal — as articulated by the pastor — is simply hospitality.

Two comments capture the spirit of the parish. An occasional visitor, a journalist, remarked, "I am not a member of the parish, but I have been an observer. Father Jodi has the legacy of a caring predecessor who left a parish that was neither moribund nor torn apart with internal issues. Blessed Sacrament parishioners have a long history of socializing together. Training and empowerment are the keys to lay involvement." And a parishioner noted, "Father Jodi listens well and really encourages us. It's not, 'Oh go ahead, if you want to.' He also furnishes the tools to get things done."

Parishes can fill personal needs like offering hospitality to the family moving with the breadwinner's job, but Blessed Sacrament Parish offers more. While it focuses on the warmth of belonging, it also challenges members to reach out to the length and breath of the human community.

While it does not organize the parish into smaller units of greater intimacy, its hospitality is the matrix from which spontaneous groups are spawned.

The Need for Community

Our deepest desire in life is for the intimacy of communion. Superbowl Sunday, the World Series, a Springsteen festival or a Saturday night at a crowded singles' bar are all events and places where we seek the warmth of human breath while we share common symbols.

When the game is over, the festival cherished as a memory, the people at the gathering dispersed, we may feel the pangs of loneliness. The events were energizing. We felt ourselves a part of something larger than ourselves — part of a crowd where we experienced a feeling of togetherness.

But this is not being part of a community which presumes continuity and a history of shared goals, struggles, and the experience of what life can be at its best.

We experience a loneliness that is the underside of an America always on the move. It may be better described as an uncertainty, restlessness or instability, a sense that something is happening to the crowd that is not happening to us. It's part of our heritage. We have images from the theater screen of the covered wagon crossing the country carrying the pioneers of American life to open new territory and settle it.

Now the large moving vans we pass on the expressways are the modern version of the covered wagon. They contain the family possessions of the executive whose company has promoted him, or the tradesman whose skills are needed elsewhere.

We are a nation on wheels, but we are not a nomadic tribe. We leave our roots behind us. The choice to move is most often dictated by economic and psychic survival. Often we choose to move because of a promotion which offers more money and a different status. Or we move because an industry has closed and the options are idleness and welfare or moving to an area where there are jobs available. Our social and economic system keeps us on wheels. A century ago Thoreau wrote, "Things are in the saddle and they ride mankind."

The itinerant family can create instant friendships at each stop, but not a community that offers nurture and stability. That kind of support only comes from roots that have been cultivated for years. The neighborhood community and the family ties with their webs of relationships are not as high a value as a more affluent lifestyle with the privacy and space an increased income can afford.

> We have been drawn toward cities large and complicated enough to meet our economic desires, and toward families small and portable (and even disposable) enough to make mobility possible. Popular sociology portrays us as victims of these "movements" and "trends," as if the woes that accompany modernity had been forced upon us. But no. The destruction of intimate community has been at our own hands. It has corresponded to our own hierarchy of values. My point is not that large cities and small families are wrong, both clearly have their values. My point is that those values stand largely in tension with the value of total and intimate community. As much as we yearn for community, we yearn even more for the social and economic prizes individual mobility can bring.[1]

The elders of Italian enclaves in urban America have much to teach the tourists who walk through those neighborhoods — on Hanover Street in Boston's North End, in the park in front of St. Leonard's, or near SS. Peter and Paul Church in San Francisco. The elders sit on park benches, play bocci ball and enjoy life. It has not passed them by. They are living it. This is not the place for a therapist to find clients.

Mental health is the by-product of a community life where people can share their stories in a leisurely fashion with people they have shared their lives with for decades.

The people who pass them on their lunch hour, well groomed and urbane, climbing the executive ladder, fearful of their competitors with whom they may be sharing the same office and the same luncheon table, are less likely to have someone with whom they can share their story. The loss of some privacy is the price of being cared for and included in the community.

> With the breakdown of the common life came growing personal disintegration and the need for a therapy which did not depend on community! . . . This theme pervades other areas of modern life. Education is a notable example. Historically, education and community were inseparable. The content of education reflected the community consensus, and at the same time helped the community evolve and perpetuate itself. Today education has become a training ground for competition, rooted in the assumption that community is gone and we must learn to stand on our own two feet. In fact, more than a training ground, education itself has become a com-

petitive arena where winners and losers are determined even before the contest is scheduled to begin.[2]

The individualism that has given Americans their strong sense of selfhood, self-determination and self-reliance must be affirmed as a positive aspect of our culture. However, this individualism has invaded American religious life leading to an emphasis on pastoral counseling at the expense of community involvement. Psychologically orientated sermons that keep the focus on feelings and personal conversion come at the expense of the mediation of God's grace flowing through shared life in community. The experience of the otherness of God savored in worship tends to get lost.

The psychological awareness in our culture must be affirmed and woven into homilies that keep the focus on the transcendent, the worship of God.

> Pastoral care leaders for the most part see the need for a corrective rather than a wholesale spurning of psychology. They appeal for a better sense of balance and express reservations about the extent to which modern therapies should displace the church's ancient cures and wisdom. Most also acknowledge that the rise of psychology took place in part because churches had so often substituted

austere moralisms or pious platitudes for vital spiritual care.[3]

The Parish As Community

The major focus of parish as community is people coming together to share events that mark their lives — births, weddings, deaths, anniversaries, graduations, illnesses, misunderstandings, shared dreams — the human experiences that touch life deeply. Collectively they are called our story. In sharing these stories over a period of years we build trust and become a community.

Community is friendship writ large. In his book, *To a Dancing God*, Sam Keen estimates that it takes five years just to seed a single friendship.

Five years (the period between moves for the average American family) is seeding-time for friendship. More time yet is required for the trust and fidelity which make for easy acceptance to ripen. Roots must intertwine, time be wasted together, crises weathered, celebrations shared before the relationship reaches maturity.

For a group to become a community the process is not essentially different. It is the shared story told in a faith community context that gets us through the shattering experiences of life.

Conducting wakes and funerals is a significant part of my profession as a parish priest. My goal is to elicit the story of the deceased from the mourners, tease them into talking about their memories. I encourage them to remember the first time they met the deceased, the events that endeared them, and the eccentric traits that brought laughter to us all. If the number of people in the funeral parlor is small, I gather them around the casket and ask them to share memories with each other.

Out of these stories I build the homily for the funeral Mass in which I interface the story of the deceased and a Jesus story. Out of the sharing of their experiences of the deceased a common story takes shape. Seen in a gospel perspective that story will be a mosaic with lights and shadows for the mourners to internalize, a source of energy long after the funeral. At every moment I am trying to rebuild or strengthen a family community. The extended family of the deceased feels itself to be a community experiencing the presence of the risen Lord for this brief moment as the casket is lowered into the grave.

All communities are intermediate social groups that both nurture their members and have a collective influence on their environment.

The country club and singles' bar focus on nurture. The political organization may nurture, but its goal is to influence the body politic.

A parish is different. Nurture and community outreach are at its core, but it is the faith dimension of the community that makes it essentially different.

St. Monica on the BART

On a weekday morning in Lent, I sat in the rear of a modern California Eastbay church to celebrate the Eucharist. To my surprise about 100 people were there, many of them women whose husbands had hustled that morning to Orinda to catch the BART at 7:22. The train would bring them to the San Francisco high-rise office district, where they would sit behind executive desks in three-piece suits. Among the 100 people were a few men, retired executives or those in the painful process of job change.

When Mass was over people milled around the vestibule where the volume of chatter suggested that the women had formed significant relationships through gathering after Mass each morning. I was invited to join a dozen of the women for breakfast and learned that each morning they gather for theological reflection on the scriptures as well as to exchange bits and pieces of information about what is going on in the community. My surface impression was that this Eastbay breakfast club had many of the elements of a Latin American *communidad de base*. After breakfast I asked the pastor, Father Brian Joyce, to tell the St. Monica story:

"I have a commitment to a parish community that has a sense of ownership." He explained that when he arrived almost six years ago he arranged for 45 home Masses throughout the parish, which provided the opportunity for parishioners to express their hopes for the parish. Out of this came a parish consultative body that held a "town meeting" where the findings from the home meetings were presented. "Then we met for another day and a half, set goals, and formed task forces that gave people a sense of ownership.

"Preaching and adult education are my gifts," he explained. "Since we had a concentration of executives in the parish, I set up luncheon sessions in downtown San Francisco and Oakland on the Fridays of Advent and Lent to discuss how the gospel and the bishops' peace and economic pastorals spoke to their work life."

Father Joyce thinks highly of the American Catholic laity. "Yes, there is consumerism and individualism, but the laity is not overwhelmed by it and given the right framework laypeople will respond to the pastorals."

He pointed out that at the luncheon meetings the men criticized the economic pastoral, particularly the section on poverty, for not being specific enough. "The peace pastoral had tremendous support, almost 700 signed the freeze petition. I used the homily time one Sunday to summarize the document and then we held workshops. They are politically conservative but open to the bishops."

The parish has a number of people who work with the poor in a West Oakland project, which he says demands a lot of their skills. "We budget a significant part of our income for projects outside the parish, but also believe that giving should involve more than money. It should be hands-on, working side by side with the people in the area.

"It forces people to ask questions about the economy. We have top executives who are very sensitive to these questions but feel that the best way for them to help the poor is to improve the economy thus providing jobs. It sounds like a trickle down response. I would like to think they would bring this kind of social analysis to the board rooms and places where decisions about the world economy are made. Frankly, it may be there, but I don't see it, at least at the hands-on caring level which is so evident among them in working with and caring for the poor in West Oakland."

One of the surprises to Father Joyce was a group of 20 men who wanted to meet for breakfast every Saturday morning to discuss the Sunday readings as well as business and personal issues. A few of the men got into the group because they were facing early retirement and were looking for support.

"This group now has a life of its own and is the only parish group that is exclusively male," explains Father Joyce. "There has been no discussion of involving their wives, although some of the men designed a one-time prayer clinic on a Saturday for six men and six women. They found it exciting — discussing and experimenting with a number of prayer forms."

St. Monica's has no parish school, "nor do I want one," says Joyce. "My fear is that if we had one we would not be able to emphasize these other areas. I see the school fund raisers in the neighboring parishes. If we had a school, the people on our social concerns committees are the kind who would be taking care of the fund raisers for the school. In the neighboring parishes I see an 'in' group focusing on the school and an 'out' group having nothing to do with the school."

The parish has no base communities in the Latin American sense, although the pastor sees some similarities in the way the Filipinos in the area unite in fraternal organizations that seem to envelop all parts of their lives.

"Americans do it through committees," he says. "We have people who are members of our parish council, liturgy and social concerns committees which interlock and network. They establish deep relationships among themselves. We form committees that tend to take a long time to strategize about issues. The divorced, the separated and the grieving meet, bonding through temporary concerns, with people moving on and new ones coming aboard. Through all of our groups we do form networks in which people can find a place."

The RCIA and liturgy are significant building blocks in St. Monica's. RCIA has a core team of eight people, a stable, small group that functions for nine months a year. Members stay on for three or four years, so the team has an identity. But members are not expected to stay on for longer than that because of the work load and the repetition. The pastor has found that Catholics who were formed in the traditional model view the RCIA with a tinge of envy saying, "I wish I had an experience like that." He has also tried the RCIA model with returning Catholics, but it has not generated the same level of commitment.

"Liturgy is central to parish life," explains Father Joyce. "It raises awareness of social issues and it opens us up to the scriptures. But its greatest value is to communicate that we are a welcoming, hospitable community. A visitor once remarked, 'There is a sense of welcome, hospitality and warmth here.' We take it for granted. It is not articulated. It is the style of our people."

Notes

1. Parker J. Palmer, *The Promise of Paradox* (Notre Dame, Indiana: Ave Maria Press, 1980), p. 69.

2. Ibid. pp. 70-71.

3. Kenneth A. Briggs, "The Wedding's Off," *Notre Dame Magazine*, Winter 85/86, p. 24.

Chapter Two

Liturgy: The Central Parish Experience

The Jesus Story is told in an endless variety of ways: a bedtime story with a child, a recognition of Jesus in the breaking of the bread, an intimate conversation with a friend, a hospitable act to a stranger, a bible discussion or participation at a Sunday liturgy.

In the Introduction I stated that the parish that tells the Story well must be strong in three areas: liturgy, formation and outreach. Each must reinforce the other two. No Catholic parish is just a liturgical parish. Liturgy is one facet of parish life, one of the ways for telling the Story. It is the formal way of "gathering the folks, telling the Story and breaking the Bread."

In this chapter, however, I confine the telling of the Story to the traditional Catholic Sunday liturgy and focus on parishes with vital liturgies. In every town and village in Catholic countries the Sunday liturgy is the sacred public event of the week. At the gathering place the telling of the Story is done through music, drama, poetry, art, architecture, words and processions. Ritual carries the freight of centuries of tradition.

A number of years ago I went to Montreal to interview theologian Charles Davis. His insights about the liturgy, old and new, are timeless:

> Liturgy is not something that can exist isolated from the surrounding culture. If you're going to have liturgy, you are going to have to use language, music, poetry, gestures, and these are taken from the surrounding culture; so the liturgy that you can have is a cultural form, depending on the state of the culture. It would be silly to hold either the liturgists or bishops responsible for the situation. The subculture on which it rested was breaking down. Consequently, the liturgy the people owned, the old liturgy, was not going to survive because of cultural factors. On the other hand it was impossible to create something that would adequately replace it.
>
> We have gone through the worst period, but it still seems almost impossible to go to a liturgical celebration where the celebrant and other participants have a confi-

dence in the power of the ritual itself and do not think it necessary to precede everything with a long explanation. There is no feeling for ritual itself. This reaches the worst manifestation in the homilies. Even when their content, intellectually speaking, is good, they are done in a way that gives one a sacred shudder.

The ritual demands a certain kind of objectivity. A homilist is not someone subjecting the congregation to his own personality, trying to reach some kind of interpersonal relationship with the congregation. He is there to perform a sacred function, to present the Word. Instead we get these repellent personal chats which are completely out of place in a sacred celebration.

The music is another thing. It has been taken over quite uncritically from modern culture. Musically speaking it is "corn." There is no quality, no tension. It plays on the emotions. It expresses yearnings crudely. Quite bluntly, it is adolescent. Young people cannot experience the richness or tension of life: that can only come as one matures. It is not apt for expressing the sacred.

Where Young Adult Catholics Meet

I received a call from Minnesota asking where visitors to Chicago could go for a good

Sunday liturgy. Although I had never been there, without hesitation I said "St. Clement's." I decided to experience its liturgy myself. I picked the Sunday during the Fourth of July weekend, the hottest of the year, a Sunday on which only people with an internalized sense of Sunday obligation would come to Mass. I was dead wrong. When I arrived, 40 or 50 young adults were clustered in small groups outside the church, a scene one might see in a rural parish where people met only on Sundays. The Mass they had attended had long ended. I was coming for the next. When I entered the church for the next Mass I saw only young adults. I sighed. "Where have all the old folks gone?" A recent parish census showed the average parishioner was a female, aged 26.

The liturgy at St. Clement's had all the right things and none of the wrong things which Davis mentioned. It was public worship rather than an appeal to the emotions. The focus was on the Word, not on personal encounter with self or the people in the pews. The music had tension. Young people could enter the depths as a relief from their professional and social lives. It was an oasis in the middle of a city, a well where one could draw from the depths of oneself and one's tradition.

After Mass I met a young journalist whom I had known before she left her parental home. "I am going to call your parents and tell them I caught you at Mass," I chided her. "You are supposed to be rebelling against your heritage. Your parents will be shocked." Actually, young people come to St. Clement's to meet other young people and to worship together. It brought me back to the southwest side of Chicago in the '50s where thousands of young Catholics met for Sunday evening dances at the St. Sabina Community Center. Some things change and yet remain the same.

The pastor, Father John Fahey, insists that St. Clement's is not a liturgical showcase. He sees the parish as a place where people in a geographic area come together for a variety of reasons, as in every parish in the country. While the parish may attract people from outside the area, his focus is on the regulars. The Sunday attendance is between 1,500 and 2,000.

"When I came here 11 years ago I walked the streets with regularity to get a feel for each neighborhood," he explained. There are six hospitals within walking distance of the rectory, and these institutions plus a Catholic university bring an array of medical and educational personnel, patients and visitors into the area. It is one of the most densely populated areas in the country with a zero housing vacancy rate.

"People live here by choice," says Father Fahey, "and leave the area with great reluctance, whether it is young people being transferred to San Francisco, families who move to the suburbs because of space, or even elderly people leaving for Arizona or a nursing home. We have the entire socioeconomic range from subsidized public housing to $300,000 condos. St. Clement's is a tough neighborhood that survived the Valentine Massacre of 1929, which is now the site of our public housing development. It's a neighborhood with character and a vital socioeconomic environment."

In the midst of this diversity is the 80-year-old St. Clement's, founded as a German national parish, and five years later changed to a territorial parish. A high degree of stability was provided by having only two pastors in its first 60 years. The sisters, running a grade school and high school until 1975 (the parish still supports a grade school), contributed to that stability. Through the years the Filipino population grew, and in the last 15 years it has become a neighborhood of single people, particularly young professionals. "We have a quality of adaptability peculiar to a living organism, drawing life from the environment, adapting to the soil and atmosphere," says Father Fahey.

As pastor his first step was working with the other people already on staff and attracting new people who could work together. For Father Fahey, the key is adaptability. "Since we are working with parishioners of such varied backgrounds, we need to have people on our staff with compatible differences." Since the parish is predominantly single with many professional women, having a woman on the staff was essential. Rather than narrowly define her responsibilities in terms of nursing homes or religious education, he encouraged her to do everything that the ordained do, church law permitting. "Since then we have added two other women to our staff plus a music director and a female principal in the elementary school."

Father John believes that St. Clement's liturgies are "the most significant point of our relationship with our people. The homilies, the music, the environment and everything that supports the liturgy is a very high priority with us. The quality of the liturgy is central to our development. It is what people find nourishing."

He also believes that the liturgy will function differently in different kinds of communities. "I worked for a number of years at a black parish that had excellent music and preaching, but our liturgy at St. Clement's is different. The throng of young people who live in the St. Clement's neighborhood, literally thousands, in large measure come from a very strong Catholic educational background in places like Notre Dame, St. Mary's, DePaul or Loyola. They come here experiencing independence in a new way. They have been away from their families for six or eight years. They have also moved away from the surrogate family they formed at college. Their identity had been defined by family or educational institutions, and now separated from that, they begin to look for something they had not realized was lost.

"When we become aware of what we lost, we begin to look for it in the places we remember having had it," says Father John. "If they find a vitality here, a sense of joy in Catholicism, in the faith, all of these earlier influences begin to come alive again. We are simply permitting people to understand their faith in a way that they never really could before. Out of it comes a trust that this is a place where one feels at home, the beginnings of community."

Father John believes community builds when hurting people meet hurting people. This can happen in the choir, or at the social after the

11:15 Mass. Gradually people move beyond their hurts and move into programs like Amnesty International, our shelter for the homeless, and different efforts to identify with women's issues. "It comes out of our homilies and associations that begin at liturgy," he says. "While our sense of community perhaps is rooted here, it is not limited to St. Clement's. We have a Peace and Justice Commission which keeps the parish in touch with the issues." The church basement is a shelter for about 30 people a night. It was developed by a dozen people from the parish and from three Protestant churches. About 250 people volunteer to stay one full night a month.

"I see this linked to the liturgy, where we speak about community and encourage people to sign up for projects. One woman said, 'For me, the whole church has simply been turned upside down. When I now come to the front of the church to receive communion, I think of the people who came to me for a cup of coffee and for a warm meal. Communion upstairs has meaning for me that it didn't have before, because of my experience with the homeless downstairs.' "

Hundreds of people are involved in the St. Clement's services. They bring people together out of a sense of religious interest. The parish has an associate who has a rich background in liturgy, and services are done carefully and meticulously so that the liturgies are prayerful and pull people into them in a powerful way. "All of us — lay people, priests, non-ordained ministers — are powerfully affected by our celebration of the liturgy," he explains.

"When we talk about liturgy, we are not talking simply about the ceremony. It is the planning of the ceremony and the catechesis that goes on for all the sacraments that is so important. The planning itself is a profound experience."

The baptism and confirmation programs are seen as a form of evangelization. Parents who have their children baptized come for three Sunday afternoons of preparations where the basics of Christianity and church are covered. The parents are seen as people having left their families a few years ago and now wondering whether some of their earlier convictions might not have more meaning than they once thought. The birth of a child is a natural time for this reassessment, and many of the parents who go through the baptismal program really become a part of the community.

The catechumenate program is in the hands of a committee that works with a staff member, and it follows the RCIA model as carefully as possible. The parish also has a Homecoming program for people who were Catholics at one time in their life, but became distant or alienated. It is in the hands of people who were in previous Homecoming programs.

"A community," Father John says, "with such diverse functions needs to offer skills training to those who perform them in the name of the community. Lay ministry training is one of our top priorities. Instead of simply using the talents the people brought we felt we owed it to them and to the church to develop their sense of lay ministry. We have a two-year program where people meet 20 times a year for training, reading, prayer and to develop a sense of their own ministry."

Father John discovered from his initial walking through the streets that the parish has a higher than average percentage of gays. "We are sensitive in our homilies about the way we talk about relationships. We don't draw our examples from the nuclear family or use anecdotes that would only fit a suburban parish. We draw upon the experiences of singles, divorced, gays and alcoholics — and do it explicitly. These are people among us who know something about the faith that the rest of us have no access to. They are not problems but prophets in our midst who have something to say to us. People pick up the message and feel comfortable."

Father John feels there is a real opportunity for small group associations in the parish because of the diversity of people's lives. "One of our great small group efforts was through a fund raiser for the renovation of the church. A woman who used the political model of our area organized 700 people to meet in numerous small group coffees." The reality is that there are many small communities in the parish, which are not organized or monitored. Through the interaction of the hundreds of parishioners deeply committed to making the liturgies profound prayerful experiences, and the outreach and social action projects that challenge cultural values, relationships are formed which need not be structured by the parish organization. Father Fahey concludes, "The parish is a base community, or at least a base from which small, informal communities are formed."

Our Lady Gate of Heaven

Jeffery Manor is a housing subdivision that departs from the grid patterns of look-alike Chicago neighborhoods. Its single-family homes are built on streets that curve and lead to cul-desacs, homes that were built by a prominent Catholic subdivision developer who also donated land for the parish complex of Our Lady Gate of Heaven.

In the midst of the development are the low-slung parish buildings — a church nestled in a school basement, a convent, and a rectory that looks like a home. The architecture departs from the immigrant neighborhood cathedrals pointing to the otherness of God. Our Lady Gate of Heaven structures point to God in family and neighborhood.

The parish became a mecca for the Catholic family that was established long enough to acquire a down payment and a 6 percent mortgage, and secure enough to continue having children on decent blue-collar wages.

However, in a few years the ideal parish for white, second-generation ethnics became the home of black families testing their acceptance into a new territory and a new parish. The change from a medium-size city parish that emphasized delivering the sacraments to a largely white, Catholic constituency, to a black population that was only 6 percent Catholic and had no deeply ingrained Catholic family traditions, was a challenge. A different kind of parish was needed, one closer to house churches of the early church.

The young staff responded with vision and vigor to the challenge of founding another parish using the same buildings. An excellent school faculty responded to blacks in search of excellence for their children. With an adequate supply of priests, sisters, seminary field-education students, and black lay teachers, Our Lady Gate of Heaven has focused on evangelization via Catholic education — maintaining a first-class parochial school and welcoming the new parishioners it has attracted into parish life. The blacks have responded positively to the school and it has been an easy step for them to assume leadership roles in the parish.

Lay leadership at Our Lady Gate of Heaven is equated with lay ownership. A leadership council brought together a variety of talents including several women with professional management skills and a successful builder. The council is formed on a model of discipleship that focuses on building community rather than being a board of directors that focuses on budgets, fund raising, and building and grounds maintenance. It involves itself with such concerns as parish apathy, neighborliness, involvement of school parents in the parish, vocations and outreach.

A black church can be an imitation white

church or it can launch out into the deep and become culturally black, understanding the gospel
as black Catholics do. This means seizing upon
public events that touch blacks as a people. In
the spring of 1980, 26 black children were mur-
dered in Atlanta by a mysterious killer who ter-
rorized the entire black community. During Holy
Week the children of Our Lady Gate of Heaven
made crosses which they carried in procession to
a field where they temporarily planted them. On
Holy Saturday men dug holes and poured the
concrete for permanent places for the crosses.
The Easter liturgy began in the field of crosses
where the scriptures were proclaimed and the
people reflected on the mystery of evil.

The breakthrough in moving from white to
black liturgy at Our Lady Gate of Heaven came
when a parishioner went to a summer workshop
on black liturgy. It was led by blacks who had
written African gospel music and led black gospel choirs. She then became liturgical director
and leader of the newly formed gospel choir.
People who experience liturgy at the parish for
the first time say "I did not know that Catholics
worshiped like this."

In 1982 a sister joined the parish staff who
was interested in the catechumenate (Rite of
Christian Initiation of Adults or RCIA) as the cor-

nerstone of renewal. For true believers the catechumenate can be the equivalent of the Second
Coming for a parish. It demands that the assembly become a teaching community, introducing
the uninitiated not only to books and seminars,
but to a Christian community in action. The
community in turn sees itself as teacher and asks
itself serious questions about its understanding
of Christian community.

"The people joining the church are a mirror
for us," pastor Father Thomas Cima observes. "It
gives us a way to check out their questions, but
also to understand who we are as a parish community. It is a dynamic designed to engage the
entire community with a new group searching
for a spiritual home as the church lives the full liturgical cycle each year." At Our Lady Gate of
Heaven, the catechumenate averages from 25 to
30 candidates a year, which has boosted church
membership at a rate of 10 percent a year for the
past three years.

One major source of candidates for the catechumenate is a required course in Catholic doc-
trine for the parents of non-Catholic school children. Although the pastor objected to this
measure, the parish leadership council insisted.
They saw parents who wanted to skip the instruction courses as freeloaders. Many of the

parents who take the required course go on to join the RCIA program.

While the catechumenate is central to the new Our Lady Gate of Heaven, Father Tom does not think it is effective unless "the other parts are in place." The Catholic school, the leadership council and the liturgy are essential, but the parish has to be established in the world around it.

Our Lady Gate of Heaven is a significant member of the larger region which is predominantly Hispanic. The neighborhood organization engages in the struggle to maintain adequate police, fire, sanitation and housing services. In the process it must challenge the government and business establishments, large and small. When parishioners engage in the political process, they come to understand that only systemic change and eternal vigilance will remedy the problems of their neighborhood.

Our Lady Gate of Heaven is a parish of young families. How does it manage lay involvement of parents with two and three jobs and young children? How does it manage not to destroy family life and cause burnout among those who tend to be involved all the time? "It is amazing how black women find time," says staff member Linda Jung. "Our attention is primarily focused on family things that allow them ways to involve their children at the same time. Yesterday was Superbowl Sunday. The men's club sponsored a Superbowl party in the parish hall and put up a big TV screen. Families brought chicken dinners and had a chance to visit with other families. Other activities include children's choirs and buses of families going to events scheduled by the Mothers' Club. Our social service ministry is run from the rectory where volunteers come with their kids to do the packaging and distribution. And the catechumenate provides a baby-sitting service while the adults are at meetings."

Although Our Lady Gate of Heaven is adequately staffed now — one priest, one professional lay staff member, plus four parishioners who have become part of the extended staff — can it face further retrenchment of professional staff?

Linda Jung, the full-time staffer, answered that "we would have to change our expectations of ministers and parish functions. We would have to sort out what we want to keep and what we are willing to let go. We are preparing for that day, but we are not making any projections. We talk about empowering the laity but we do not always give them the necessary skills. We give them the freedom to act but not always the training. The time they manage for parish and com-

munity amazes me, given their commitment to
family and jobs.

"Our strength is that we are small," she explains. "And because we are small, we have become a community, a house church with subdi-
visions that could be called base communities.
The key is accountability to one another and caring for one another. People come on Sunday because they want to be here."

Chapter Three

Christian Formation

Every corporation, social club and political party has an orientation or training program that culminates in a ritual of acceptance. Churches are no exception. The traditions are deeply embedded in the life of each denomination. Within Christian churches formation of adults concludes with the rite of baptism.

In the Catholic church the traditional method of introducing new members was through formal convert classes or one-on-one instruction. The community made little attempt at evangelization or outreach. When a standard textbook was completed, the person was baptized or formally received into the Catholic church. It was presumed that the neophyte would simply pick up the spirit and life of Catholicism from the community.

Although there was no mentor or identifiable support system to bring the person into the community, the cohesiveness of the neighborhood and the parish seemed adequate. Socialization took place through things that defined the Catholic subculture — no meat on Friday, the obligation to attend Sunday Mass, and marriage and divorce regulations. It also took place through the institutionalization of basic human services: Catholic schools, hospitals, cemeteries, and a network of parish and regional organizations.

This socialization process became unglued when Pope John XXIII responded to the "signs of the times" by opening the windows of the church and letting the breeze of change blow through.

The ghetto walls had already been severely cracked as young people attended colleges and universities, went to work in a pluralistic society and acquired the affluence that allowed them to travel and participate in a broader world. People were forced to ask themselves why they were Catholic, and many became aware that it had no meaning for them outside their subculture.

The Story no longer had a context. Where there was no evangelization and outreach, there was no effective formation. The Story was no longer life-giving.

The RCIA

Recognizing this, the Vatican Congregation for Divine Worship issued the Rite of Christian Initiations of Adults (RCIA) in 1972. It is a contemporary version of the ancient catechumenate which prepared neophytes for the initiation rites of baptism, confirmation, and first Eucharist which in the early church were done in the context of the entire community.

In spite of retaining ancient words — "scrutinies" and "mystagogia" — RCIA is a new process in the American Catholic parish that is focused on building community.

> The initiation of catechumens takes place step by step in the midst of the community of faithful. Together with the catechumens, the faithful reflect upon the value of the paschal mystery, renew their own conversion, and by their example lead the catechumens to obey the Holy Spirit more generously.[1]

American Catholic parishes like the RCIA, not because it has been mandated, but because it speaks to the pastoral void that parish staffs have experienced in bringing people into the community. It affords the possibility of renewing parish life. The key to its success is the RCIA team or staff, the sponsors, and other parishioners. The catechetical methodology is based on faith sharing. The emphasis is on the catechumens assimilating the faith of the community and the community in turn being challenged by the faith of the catechumens. Although the RCIA is not a program, it has stages through which the catechumens must pass.

While the Easter vigil is the focus for the ritual celebration of joining the community, the RCIA has a before and an after. Early in Lent the bishop ritualizes the reception into the catechumenate. The catechumens gather at the cathedral from every corner of the diocese to experience a dimension of church they cannot experience in their local community. In the "mystagogia" — after the Easter vigil — they have the opportunity to discuss the presence of the Spirit in their lives and accept the challenge to be witnesses to this same Spirit.

This does not happen automatically. In the hands of a staff that does not have the larger view of a parish as a community, the RCIA can become a gimmick. Dr. Ralph Keifer offers this challenge to the parish that is putting new wine into old wine skins:

> It is a church incapable of initiating, because it is incapable of living and acting as a community of faith into which people can be initiated. As we stand at present, people can be

partially assimilated but they cannot be initiated . . . the new initiatory rites are, for all
practical purposes, impotent, because those
who use them are the products and shapers
of that very same culture. If we continue to
accept this cultural drift, we will use the new
initiatory rites, just as we have used everything else in the Roman books, grudgingly,
and with no attempt to form a community of
faith which might be fit to celebrate them. Instead, we will continue with the vain hope
that education will do the job.[2]

The points Dr. Keifer makes reinforce the
thesis of this book, namely, that the RCIA is effective when there is a welcoming community
and the community itself has a prophetic dimension that challenges both itself and the neophytes.

St. Clare of Montefalco

St. Clare of Montefalco is an older parish in
the Gage Park section of Chicago, a focus of the
civil rights marches led by Martin Luther King in
1968.

It had been a slumberland parish providing
the essential services to its members until a
young pastor arrived in 1977 and won the people
over with his smile, his lightheartedness and his
caring.

According to Father James Friedel, his associate and then his successor, "Father Bill represented a symbolic change from the way things were. Gaining the trust of the people the first year was painful. We wanted to get past the gas station approach to parish life with the people getting filled up but feeling no warmth. We began responding to hurts by establishing a ministry for the divorced, an AA group, Alanon, and other recovery groups. We broadened involvement and helped empower the people by helping them participate as lectors, commentators and ushers."

The RCIA has been a key to parish renewal. According to Associate Pastor Father Joseph McCormick, the RCIA's reason for being is "welcoming people in the community. But once it was established it became a source of renewal for the entire parish.

"The old method of the priests giving private or classroom instructions has changed," he explains. "Now a significant segment of the parish instructs and welcomes the newcomer. This Easter we had only three to be initiated into the church, but we have other categories of people in the program: inactive Catholics, people baptized without any formation, and adults to be confirmed."

The St. Clare catechumenate community has 35 people who are actively involved in the process as sponsors, lay catechists, leaders of faith sharing groups, hospitality and outreach programs. Monthly meetings are held to which all are invited, including the candidates of previous years.

"When a person comes to the rectory to meet a priest to talk about becoming a Catholic or an active member of our parish, I interview the person to find out if RCIA is what they need. I explain the RCIA process, the small faith-formation groups that meet in homes, the monthly gatherings for everyone and the role of the sponsor. If there is agreement, I put the person in contact with a sponsor committee that will pick a sponsor for the candidate. At that point I could drop out. The catechumenate community takes over."

The parish is developing a pool of 12 or 15 sponsors who will take turns, and hopefully prevent burnout.

A candidate does not wait until fall, when a large group is formed, but immediately becomes a part of an existing group, or a new group is started. Father McCormick explains that two or three is enough. Two candidates each need a sponsor and, with a catechist, "this in itself becomes a small community. We can have two or three groups going at one time."

Candidates are brought into the worshiping community (Sunday liturgy) right away, although they leave after the homily during Advent and Lent. They go to a room in the rectory, where they discuss the Word with their sponsors and learn to use the lectionary as a simple tool for scripture sharing. "After they read a passage, the leader has a few well-crafted questions that evoke some personal experience one can place aside the Jesus Story. Or they are simply asked to pick an image or word that moves them. Or they are asked, 'If you took this passage seriously, what would it cost you?' It is very simple."

The parish community of St. Clare's is a corporate sponsor for the candidate or inactive Catholic. Even parishioners who might have an interest in the subject of the monthly catechumenate meeting are invited. These meetings begin with song, a prayer and a scripture reflection, and as many as 35 attend.

Some of the long-time parishioners are confused by the catechumenate and admit they do not always understand what is going on. But many say they enjoy it and get more out of it than the catechumens. In this way the candidates unknowingly challenge the members of the community about their faith. Says Father McCormick, "I see our sponsors and catechists develop in self-confidence as well as in the depth of their faith commitment. The catechumens do have a ministry to the church. They challenge us in our understanding of our faith as a public witness. Entering the church in a public way challenges all. It causes people to ask themselves if their faith is only something between themselves and Jesus."

The parish response is varied. Some members say it is beautiful. Some feel cheated that they did not have this formation. Some feel that the Sunday liturgies that focus on the catechumens are an intrusion. Others know that something important is happening at the altar and are happy that these people are in a conversion process.

At one of the parish Easter vigils the congregation was invited to greet and welcome the newly baptized members. There was a surprising outburst of welcome. People, acting contrary to their blue-collar, conservative, big-city culture came up to the newly baptized to shake their hands and hug them. An elderly woman said, "Never did I think I would come to church and hug a complete stranger."

"The outreach dimension of the RCIA takes

place in the mystagogia phase after Easter when we look at Spirit life in parish and in the world," Father McCormick explains. "We present and invite them to take part in parish ministries. We introduce them to Bread for the World and Pax Christi groups active within the parish. Also they are asked to look at their work as a challenge to give public witness to their faith."

The RCIA is one element that makes St. Clare's a warm and welcoming community. The network of relationships among the 35 members of the catechumenate, plus the network generated by the Renew program and outreach projects, has an effect on the worship service. When a large number of people in these networks come to Sunday liturgy, they are quick to feel the presence of others with whom they share life at a deep level. This builds as the Eucharistic service unfolds.

RENEW

In 1979, two Newark diocesan priests, Father Thomas Kleissler, steeped in the small group experience of the Christian Family Movement, and Father Thomas Ivory, with a passionate conviction about the newly sanctioned adult catechumenate (RCIA) as a basis for parish renewal, put together a program called RENEW.

Since then it has spread across the country like wildfire.

The small groups in this model listen together to a reading and share their faith stories in five six-week units in each other's homes over a period of two and a half years.

Where once faith was an individual affair, this process became a step toward a community-based faith. Faith sharing in small groups can be threatening to middle-aged and older people raised in a church of unquestioning faith and absolute doctrines. RENEW gave them a way to begin rethinking their concept of parish. They could meet people they had before only nodded to at Sunday liturgies and share more deeply in their faith. This in turn was a step toward making liturgy more of a community event.

RENEW is a three-year program to which the staff and leadership of the parish must make a firm commitment of time and energy. The first year is spent preparing the parish for the units in spring and fall semesters. On sign-up Sunday at the beginning of each semester one is only making a commitment to a six-week segment, giving everyone a graceful way of bowing out at the end of any unit. The units are structured to take people through graded stages, designed to lead people to RENEW'S understanding of discipleship and commitment to living the gospel.

RENEW nudges its participants toward concern for social issues. James Kelly, in his article "Does the RENEW program Renew?" (*America*, March 7, 1987), writes: "RENEW does not push too hard. It encourages people to think of things on a small scale that they can do for the poor, such as running clothing drives and food drives. But RENEW is mindful of the distinction between charity and justice."

After the parishioners finish the five semesters of RENEW, people who have had a good experience often wish to continue meeting.

Kelly emphasizes that the very process of RENEW is for the church, "because it involves scores of lay leaders — women more than men. RENEW directly engages the laity in responsibility for spiritual formation, and this certainly has significance for the future church as the number of seminarians dwindles and questions about women's ordination increase. . . . RENEW explicitly aims to deepen the attachment to their parishes in a way congruent with the major themes of Vatican II."

A Vital Part of Parish Life

Along with RCIA, RENEW has become a vital part of parish life at St. Clare of Montefalco.

"Community was a category for me," explains Father Friedel. "A decade before coming to St. Clare's I visited Latin America and saw a vibrant church but also realized that the base community could not be transported as such up here. I became convinced that if we are going to pass on the message by empowering people, somehow we have to gather them together in some sort of groups or communities."

The staff at St. Clare's examined both the needs of the parish in this area and the options available. The RENEW program met their needs on several levels. The focus would be small group weekly meetings as well as large group gatherings for enrichment. RENEW provided take-home materials that could also be used in the parish bulletin.

"We liked the thematic development: looking inwardly at oneself and then reaching out to the community. It seemed to be a happy marriage between prayer life and outreach.

"This was happening at the same time we were developing a food pantry. We also hosted a Pax Christi meeting at which Dan Berrigan spoke. This was facilitated mostly by a parishioner who had wide contacts and to whom the parishioners were willing to listen, if not accept his entire liberal agenda. RENEW helped create a climate for the monthly food drive, and a shoe collection for Poland. St. Clare's is not marching on the South African embassy, but there is a programmatic consciousness raising here that we simply did not have before RENEW."

What happens when the formal RENEW program ends? St. Clare's started RENEW with about 280 people in small groups. Now that it has ended 60 or 70 people are still meeting in seven small groups.

Father Jim elaborates: "Some of them are very informal, getting together for a Christmas party or to relate to a death. Five of them meet for Lent and/or Advent. We provide outlines if they ask for them. RENEW established relationships for some who want to continue in either formal or informal ways."

St. Sylvester

Logan Square is the battleground for Chicago's Hispanic gangs. Drug trafficking, crime, and a high dropout rate for high school students are a focus for news media reporting and municipal conferences. St. Sylvester's, founded as a German church, has an imposing edifice and a commanding view of expansive Humbolt Park. I came to visit the young, first assignment associate, Father Paul Flaherty. After a casual greeting, almost as casually he continued, "We are burying a suicide tomorrow. Earlier this week I had a funeral for an 18-year-old overdose victim, a regular parishioner."

The area is 85 percent Hispanic — 50 percent Puerto Rican, 25 percent Mexican, and 10 percent Central American. The other 15 percent represent elderly Polish-Americans as well as some new Polish immigrants, and a few young white professionals. The estimated parish membership is 3,000 families of which 2,200 are registered. The unemployment rate is high and the employed work in low-paying jobs often working 16 monotonous hours a day. According to Father Paul, "This sets the stage for going crazy drinking on weekends. It reminds me of the saloons in the old Wild West movies."

What are the possibilities for spiritual formation and renewal in a parish that faces such a challenge in the lives of its parishioners? RENEW started before Father Paul arrived at the parish. There were 18 Spanish-speaking groups and six English-speaking groups. The groups kept going after RENEW, becoming faith sharing groups. The numbers have held for four years. They recruit new members each quarter, but new members come mostly by word of mouth. New people are channeled into these groups and a few develop and become leaders in the community.

Father Paul attributes the success of RENEW in this parish to the fact that it was done bilingually. "In the beginning the coordinating committee worked patiently in combating the language barrier, planning together for each language group and, in the process, forging bonds. After RENEW was finished, the bonding among these parish leaders lowered misunderstanding and built trust."

Outreach becomes a natural extension of RENEW in this parish that lives so close to the streets. "Our faith groups have a sense of being tied to the entire parish community and neighborhood. One of the actions they took as a total group was to hire a bus and ride slowly through the neighborhood. Different people would ask the bus driver to stop. They would then point out a drug dealer, a headquarters for a gang and the like. Our faith groups do not have their heads in the sand. They are painfully aware every day of the pain in Humbolt Park."

The two priests at St. Sylvester's have the herculean task of daily survival from the demands of the neighborhood. They find RENEW a vehicle for identifying people who are stable enough to want to deepen their faith and bring people together across cultural lines while preserving their cultural and ethnic heritages. RENEW helps St. Sylvester's to shape people for leadership roles in this whirlpool of cultural change.

Christ Renews His Parish

Christ the King parish in Chicago's Beverly area offers the best of the past and present. There, a black city chief of police can live comfortably alongside a third-generation Irish judge or lawyer. When word got out in the neighborhood that a boy was hit by a car and near death, there was standing room only in the church that night for a prayer service.

In 1979 the pastor, Father Edward Meyer, had a serious coronary and other health problems. In gratitude for his recovery, he wanted to offer the parish a spiritual legacy. His desire was shared by some parishioners who had made annual retreats.

They brought *Christ Renews His Parish,* a parish renewal program from Cleveland, to Christ the King. CRHP focuses on the spiritual development of a group of 18 men or women. Two groups a year go through the program, but they are not limited to a strict schedule. Time is important for the conversion process and for the scriptures to become integrated into daily living. In 1986 Christ the King was conducting its 12th group CRHP and not slowing down.

The goal is spiritual formation with a heavy emphasis on the scriptures, sharing the stories of God's interventions, the bonding that results in spiritual friendships, and closer ties with the parish community. Many of the techniques of the Cursillo movement are evident.

CRHP opens with an intense weekend at the parish complex presented by a team from the parish who have already been through the encounter. A trust level gradually develops as they go through 13 meetings which follow the weekend. Some participants are able to tell about alcohol addiction or spouse abuse in their homes for the first time. From this an outreach team is developed to do family interventions.

The effects of divorce on children surfaced and Rainbow, a program run by parishioners, was introduced to help the children. "Social justice is one of the areas we pursue," reports associate pastor, Father Dennis O'Neill. "The message gets through. After a discussion on the beatitudes, we had many judges and lawyers who asked, 'How can I live the beatitudes in a courtroom?' "

In their witness talks members are able to pinpoint God's interventions in the twists and turns of their spiritual journeys.

Christ the King has a history of being a tight community with fierce parish pride. As blacks have moved into the area they have been welcomed into the parish and recruited for CRHP. Although the area has a high Catholic density, people of other faiths join the program. Neighborhood relationships are a high priority. "We have blacks and Baptists who are able to share the tension they feel in a white, affluent, Irish community," Father Dennis continues. "The divorced, even those without annulments, move into parish eucharistic leadership roles."

I did a double take. "How come?"

"It is like Peter's experience in the house of Cornelius," concluded Father Dennis. "When you have been loving and praying with them for six months, how can you tell them they are un-worthy for ministry because they are in a second marriage?"

There are many spin-offs from CRHP. Welcoming new neighbors is as much a part of community life as keeping one's lawn trimmed. Through the 12 groups who have been in CRHP, 400 to 500 people have come to know each other in a more intimate way with the scriptures as the basis for their values. Spiritual friendships have developed. The basic values of RCIA are embedded in CRHP as it is lived out at Christ the King.

As Father Dennis moves on and the pastor takes a sabbatical in the coming year, Christ the King will have visiting priests for the liturgies. But the ministry in the parish will be done by parishioners. What was once a highly clericalized parish now because of CRHP has a laicized ministry. With hundreds of people interacting at a profound spiritual and caring level in a closely knit neighborhood, Christ the King parish may be the largest base community in the United States.

Notes

1. *Rite of Christian Initiation of Adults*, USCC, 1984, p. 1.

2. Ralph Keifer, *Made, Not Born*, "New Perspectives on Christian Initiation and the Catechumenate," Notre Dame Press, 1976, p. 148.

Chapter Four

Parishes Reaching Out

> The greatest challenge of the day is how to
> bring about a revolution of the heart, a revo-
> lution which has to start with each one of us.
> When we begin to take the lowest place, to
> wash the feet of others, to love our brothers
> and sisters with that burning love, that pas-
> sion, which led to the Cross, then we can
> truly say, "Now I have begun."
>
> *Dorothy Day*

On the wall of my office is a framed copy of
the woodcut *Christ of the Breadlines* by Quaker
artist, Fritz Eichenberg. It depicts a line of
women and men bundled in heavy outerwear,
with all but one standing with head and shoul-
ders bent from a life of defeats. The central figure
is Jesus, standing tall but pensive, his head
slightly bowed.

Eichenberg's woodcuts appeared in *The*

Catholic Worker, Dorothy Day's monthly newspaper. They were the visual images that captured in arresting form what the Catholic Worker movement was and is about. *The Catholic Worker* is the Statue of Liberty, the potent symbol for the radical American Catholic response to Matthew's call in his gospel to find the Christ on our city streets, huddled in doorways, or sleeping under viaducts.

The Catholic Worker's effectiveness was built on its selected who had to make a commitment to a radical lifestyle, wearing clothes from the clothing room, and eating food cooked for street people. One had to trust in the Lord "like the birds in the air."

Can *The Catholic Worker* tradition be duplicated in a parish setting? Perhaps not. A parish's agenda is so diversified that the *Catholic Worker* can only be the beacon calling us to approximate the gospel challenge not to care about "what tomorrow will bring." In this chapter we will look at three parish versions of this aspect of the Jesus Story.

The Gospel According to Corpus Christi

It is a rare parish that sees itself as a community of advocates of the poor and oppressed rather than focusing on the comfort of its parishioners. Such a parish transcends its boundaries. In the words of John Wesley, the world is its parish.

Corpus Christi, an inner-city parish on the outer rim of the Rochester, New York business district, has this mystic view of parish ministry, which seems as idealistic and foolish as the dreams of Jesus, Francis and Don Quixote. Corpus Christi's philosophy is that its own parishioners must be nourished and that no dreams will be realized unless the nurturing community attends to comforting one another. But it clearly believes that nurture and comfort follow, rather than precede, the Christian mission to the poor.

If comforting its members is the goal of the parish, the result will be good feelings like those experienced on a weekend with friends at a lake cottage. If afflicting the comfortable or beating people into the ground with the hard sayings of Jesus is the goal, there will be only a few diehards around to keep the doors open. Challenge and comfort are integral to the Christian community. But balance is important. How the parish tilts toward one or the other gives it its distinctive style. Corpus Christi opens its sails to the challenge.

The diocese had decided to close the granite, gothic church and its school almost on the eve of the parish's 100th anniversary. Its East Main Street neighborhood was in decay with stores boarded up and homes empty. City services declined as the poor and disenfranchised moved in.

Father Jim Callan, less than two years ordained, was given a temporary assignment there, a few months before it was scheduled to close. The charismatic young man hit the bricks running. People from the area — and for miles around — heard about his preaching and openness to the Spirit. Soon the congregation began to grow.

The new pastor declared finances a non-issue. "We don't worry about money at Corpus Christi because we don't have any," he said. Members eagerly contributed to eliminating outstanding bills including diocesan taxes. When $90,000 was needed for repairs to the school, parishioners provided the money through interest-free loans. The decision to close was stayed.

One of the perks of a clerical itinerant is free lodging at rectories. When I called to book a room at Corpus Christi the secretary said that there wasn't any. "The rectory is filled with Salvadoran refugees," she explained. The pastor intercepted the message and assured me of lodging in the home of a parishioner.

On meeting the pastor I complimented him on the clean parking lot. He seemed surprised by my opener, since the parish pays no maintenance people. It also has no cook, although someone was cooking dinner for the sanctuary people. Only the secretaries are paid. The large, full-time staff gets only an allowance for gas. Cars, homes and food are provided by parishioners.

I got into the pastor's car, a give-away from a parishioner, and wondered if it would make it around the block. We toured the properties donated to the parish, which included a drop-in storefront for the hundreds of kids in the neighborhood, a modern medical clinic operated by professional volunteers, and a house for the rehabilitation of newly released convicts associated with the parish jail ministry. The parishioners were remodeling an abandoned warehouse into a restaurant to be staffed by ex-convicts.

The parish maintains a shelter in the basement of the church. During my visit 14 street people or families were fed and nine men sheltered. This outreach program to the homeless involves a minimum of 60 parishioners. They volunteer one night a month, with two people working each night — one stays awake while the other sleeps, staying each other through the night.

Through three $50,000 gifts, a large aban-
doned building has been bought to expand these
services and two families associated with the local university have moved into it to offer more
personal attention to the people in the soup line
and continuity in care to the homeless. Plans for
a hospice for the dying are on the drawing
board.

The Corpus Christi outreach also extends to
Port-au-Prince, Haiti. Each year a group of parishioners works with Mother Teresa's Missionaries of Charity and tastes, sees and smells the
stench of poverty.

As the pastor and I broke bread in a local
restaurant, I was savoring nuggets of wisdom
from a young man who was a college rebel in the
late '60s. "I don't bother with building adminis-
tration and bookkeeping. We have people who
are competent in those areas."

The Corpus Christi staff works out of a clin-
ical-pastoral model. "I like to visit old folks and
do counseling," says Father Jim. "Priests should
do what they are best at and not bother with the
rest." But the shocker of the evening was his one
liner: "I do not see myself as a priest." After two
or three hours of conversation I was able to place
it in a context. More important than his ordination is his baptism, which puts him on equal

footing with every parishioner and staff member. This vision makes collaborative ministry possible by striking at the roots of clericalism. His authority is vested in him by the people of the neighborhood and the parishioners — as well as by his bishop.

The Corpus Christi parish assembly reminded me of a New England town meeting. The Assembly meets every six weeks and everyone is invited. Father Jim sits in the middle of the hall listening and answering questions.

Two other important centers of influence I discovered during my visit were the pulpit and the Thursday evening liturgies. While the pastor shares the pulpit with other staff members, religious and lay, the gospel message from his lips is especially vibrant and powerful — more penetrating than a two-edged sword. The Thursday evening liturgy, while unlike Sunday's, is less formal. A couple of hundred people sit on the sanctuary floor or otherwise close to the altar. It is a distinctively young assembly, quick to respond to every nuance of the liturgy. The homily cuts to the quick and is followed by a time for personal statements in the prayer of the faithful. The mood is joyful, a true community of believers and lovers. It is a strong statement about the power of the Eucharist.

Corpus Christi is a prophetic community, but it needed a genuine prophet to start the process. Now it has the possibility of continuing to remain such after Father Jim moves on. Prophetic preaching and prophetic action support each other. Liturgy and life in the community are wedded.

The Sanctuary on the Hill

This was not my first visit to St. Teresa's in the Goat Hill area in San Francisco. On past visits I had heard from the older parish members — most now dead or in nursing homes — about how the people had fled to the Goat Hill area during the great earthquake in 1906. With only the clothes on their backs and with nothing to retrieve from a destroyed city, they made their homes on the Hill.

In its prime, St. Teresa's was a solid working class parish, for folks from various ethnic backgrounds. Freeways and industrialization chipped away at the neighborhood and families moved out. Today it retains the characteristics of an enclave with a proud history and a breathtaking view of the city and the bay. And it has become an attractive urban neighborhood for young professionals.

St. Teresa's is close to the top of the Hill, a

long pull for me when I get off of bus 22. By Catholic standards 100-year-old St. Teresa's is small. The pastoral team is made up of Father Peter Sammon, who has been pastor for 15 years; and Sisters Kathleen Healy and Lucia Lodolo, pastoral associates both of whom have been there longer than the pastor. Sister Kathleen was principal of the school and Sister Lucia taught there before it was closed.

It is not a parish which one would think would be the first in the archdiocese to declare itself a public sanctuary for Central American political refugees. In coming to this decision, the parish used a process of discernment that Father Peter says was "one of the high points of my pastoral career. Its use was a great breakthrough for the parish." The decision to become a sanctuary came after a year of discussion when the parish voted 80 percent in favor.

Father Peter explains that they had to deal with a lot of negative images of foreigners and of them as law-breakers.

The process of discernment used is the same process that the bishops use in the peace pastoral to help people form their consciences. "Get the facts, ask gospel questions, and come to a decision. We brought in speakers and used the bulletin to answer questions. We told people it would be childish to vote merely to please or upset the pastor. We asked them to vote their conscience, reflecting and making their own decision. We were asking them to make an adult decision. Going through the process, we told them, was more important than how they voted."

Another key to this success was strong leadership. "We were able to bring the people along with us because of our willingness to serve them. It is pretty hard to write off 15 years of service," said the pastor. "It is arrogant to think we can form community by manipulating people through the subtle use of clerical power," he continued. "In the past people disarmed us from engaging in public issues with a moral content by saying it was political or controversial. So in the past we sat around and did nothing about the holocaust, slavery, civil rights, even apartheid today. It is important to ask the right questions. People went along with major social evils because they asked if they were legal rather than asking if they were moral or in keeping with the gospel."

Father Peter does not believe the parish could have moved on sanctuary without going through the various crises and evolutions encountered in the past 15 years. A major one was the school closing about a decade ago when the enrollment declined. While the parish lost some contact with younger families, he feels "that it was the best thing that happened to us. I no longer see a parochial school as a value. Its closing forced us to enter dialogue with the parish and put our energies into developing leadership."

Father Peter explained his ideas on leadership training at St. Teresa's: "My goal is to help people develop skills, to feel responsible and assume leadership roles in the parish, to develop a theology that supports this in their relationship with God."

Leadership evolved in the parish through the development of a parish council, a liturgy committee, and a St. Vincent de Paul Society that responded to the needs of the poor in an area housing project. "We had committees that put our finances in order and arranged parish socials. When we set parish goals in a mission statement ten years ago, we said the parish should be a sanctuary for all. Everybody is welcome here. When one of our people was questioned about why we were a sanctuary, she said, 'Sanctuary is nothing new to us. We believe a church is for all people.' "

Community organization has been an important part of the parish development. As it has moved from a church offering security and comfort to a prophetic parish, it has taken a leading role in the San Francisco Organization Project by developing small groups that push for social change. Through SFOP it forced a major grocery store to hire security guards after one of the parishioners was stabbed there. It has also cleaned up the hill and got rid of a junk yard.

"We feel that community organization is the most valuable thing we have in our pastoral training," says the pastor. "But it must be value centered. Every meeting must begin with a reflection session, a reading from scripture or the like. The organizers must have an understanding of the process, not simply specific goals."

Liturgy, RCIA, a parish council, and attempts at forming small groups are part of the infrastructure of this parish. RCIA and liturgy are life-giving. The parish has a gifted liturgy committee with subcommittees that prepare the liturgy for 24 Sundays and feasts. A lot of work goes into drafting and execution as the early drafts of the subcommittees are worked over by the full committee.

The parish did get involved with the base community model. "A number of years ago," according to Sister Kathleen, "a priest who had been in Brazil stayed here for a while and got me interested in the base community model of small communities. We adopted the Latin American model of shared prayer, scripture and a task and formed nine groups, three of which remain in some way. But the experiment only lasted a few years. We did not take time to know each other. We did not find a balance between the task and the sharing. As with the parish's early fumbling with the formation of a parish council, the staff members were doing too much. We backed off and gave the lay people breathing space."

The staff now believes that it has the right combination of task and sharing in the liturgy and on the parish council and other committees. They are seen as communities without giving them the Latin American name. These small pockets come together for liturgies and socials, and members form interlocking friendships. The model helps people get involved and support one another in community organization and sanctuary work. "A woman who was too shy to read in a group became a spokesperson in a city-wide venture," notes Sister Kathleen. "We try to make reflection a part of the community organization meetings. It is too easy to lose contact with our values in our press to take action."

Turning to a discussion of RCIA, Sister

Kathleen says it is different from the one-to-one convert model, "where I did most of the talking. We now ask converts to share their experience and we call on parishioners to share theirs with them. The converts become familiar with the parishioners and the parishioners with them. Three members of the present group want to remain a sharing group after RCIA formally ends. This says that RCIA has possibilities for becoming an American version of the base communities.

"One of my goals," explains Sister Kathleen, "is to develop a more effective use of scripture in the meeting. One method is to get the people to identify with different people in the gospel story, and apply the story to our personal lives. We also need to do a social analysis of the story as it affects the world. How does one's work militate or support the ideals of this story and what can we do about it? What comes naturally to simple people often needs a lot of preliminary work to become simple for sophisticated people. We need to develop a methodology that fits our experience. Therefore, there is a need for workshops in which you can experience a variety of methodologies."

Like Corpus Christi, St. Teresa's parish is prophetic without demanding that every parishioner get aboard. There is room for the seniors and youth group to develop their own agendas, but the invitation to look at an experience such as Central America is ever present. The liturgy is not used to support a cause. Its power is not its particularity, but its universality.

The Gospel According to Sexual Refugees

"All leave by the back door," the bus driver shouted as he pulled the bus to the curb at 18th and Castro, the gay capital of San Francisco. Holy Redeemer Church was only a few blocks away. The parish church, rectory, school and convent had been built by Irish immigrants. Now it is the Catholic parish of sexual refugees.

Father Tony McGuire, who had spent his priesthood in Hispanic communities, was asked to take the sensitive assignment of pastor.

The reasons are obvious. He is open, caring, joyful, relaxed, and possesses an obvious holiness that can only come from a deep prayer life. His older associate, Sister Cleta Harold, has a wisdom, a joy and an approachableness that comes from her security with who she is.

Father Tony and Sister Cleta are willing to deal with gays, who are often hostile to a church which they feel rejected them. But Father Tony insists that Holy Redeemer is not to be a gay parish, but a Catholic parish open to all the people in the area including a residue of elderly people and straights who would be willing to worship in a parish that is predominantly homosexual.

I came both to visit with the pastor and to take part in an ecumenical, charismatic anointing service for AIDS victims and others. The prayer style of the service was clearly charismatic in the genre of a gospel church service. An Episcopal priest, who identified himself as gay, gave the homily. The congregation had an opportunity to choose from a half dozen ministers who did the anointing, including a Catholic priest and sister. Each had a different style.

Father Tony, while not passing judgment on their lifestyle, is able to minister to gays in a world that is often hostile to them. The parish is truly Catholic with a sense of outreach to people of other cultures, religions and lifestyles.

After the service Father Tony and I talked about base communities. There is one such group in the parish composed of gays and straights, men and women. The Latin America model, which presumes some permanency, did not work at Holy Redeemer. In a highly transient area the members of the group will not bond like people who have lived in the same village for generations.

This group had to be structured for people leaving and new people coming aboard. By featuring a speaker or a scripture series during Lent, Holy Redeemer is able to invite parishioners to look the group over with a view to joining. The group meets regularly, sponsors continued scripture discussions, and arranges parties to celebrate significant events.

Holy Redeemer is a corporate witness to the gospel of Jesus Christ. It calls people to join the community at whatever level of entrance they choose. It is inclusive: young and old, gay and straight, Roman Catholic and people of other denominations. There is no trace of pity or patronization. It is presumed that everyone, including the staff, is struggling individually and as a community, to come to peace with their sexuality, their need for intimacy, for community, and for communion with God. The presence of the living God is almost tangible at Holy Redeemer.

The three stories are situated in parishes with unique constituencies. Corpus Christi, while anchored in a neighborhood, draws its members from a metropolitan area like a magnet school. It appeals to Catholics who want to live a prophetic life with a parish base.

St. Teresa's has the advantage of being small so its staff is not consumed with the sacramental rituals of a larger parish. It is in a city that is accustomed to change as a way of life.

Holy Redeemer simply happens to be located in a gay neighborhood. The staff is committed to telling the Story to people who hunger and thirst for God's Word, and to telling it in signs that relate to their pain.

When a parish puts itself on the line and is willing to suffer the agony of being counter to prevailing culture, the Sunday liturgy will convey this tension in the music, the homily, the kiss of peace. The liturgy will bring parishioners to the depths. Formation will not be a perfunctory orientation for beginners. They can see that they are being initiated into a mystery, a community that both cares and struggles with caring. Parish outreach is the source of its bonding.

Chapter Five

Base Communities

The flavor of the Jesus Story can never be captured by reading it alone. Like any other story it is best told in a community setting, its meaning best heard among friends in familiar surroundings.

A tight community of believers allows individuals the freedom to explore gospel ways of relating to the world while their bonding opens up space to explore deep places within. Mutual trust can disclose elements of the Story not evident on the printed page. It's a process that takes time, but in turn, the Story will shape the community that shares it.

The gospel cannot be taught, it can only be caught. Jesus needed the intimacy of three years with a small group of followers — a gathering of

friends amid familiar surroundings — to help
them internalize his message of salvation. He
shaped this small community by relating to the
people where they lived and worked, calling
them to bring their gifts to the task he set out for
them.

> As he was walking by the Sea of Galilee he
> saw two brothers, Simon, who was called Pe-
> ter, and his brother Andrew; they were mak-
> ing a cast in the lake with their net, for they
> were fishermen. And he said to them, "Fol-
> low me and I will make you fishers of men."
> And they left their nets at once and followed
> him. Going on from there he saw another
> pair of brothers, James son of Zebedee and
> his brother John; they were in their boat with
> their father Zebedee, mending their nets,
> and he called them. At once, leaving the boat
> and their father, they followed him (Mt 4:18-
> 22).

The formation process Jesus uses in the gospel also includes the intimacy of companionship
and hospitality:

> Jesus turned around, saw them following
> and said, "What do you want?" They an-
> swered, "Rabbi" — which means Teacher —
> "where do you live?" "Come and see," he
> replied; so they went and saw where he
> lived, and stayed with him the rest of that
> day (Jn 1:38-39).

Biblical scholars help us to reconstruct the settings in which Jesus told the Story. The gospel of Luke and its companion volume, the Acts of the Apostles, are about table fellowship, a collection of guest and host stories about the missionary ventures generated in the Spirit-led communities of Jerusalem and Antioch. Throughout, houses take on a spiritual significance, pre-dating church buildings by three centuries.

> Houses function as indispensable stages for the Lukan dramas of Mary and Martha, Jesus meeting with the Pharisees, the woman who loses and finds a coin, the prodigal son, the rich man and Lazarus and Zaccheus. . . . Luke's account of Pentecost sets the time for the real Actor of Acts, the Holy Spirit, who creates the church in a private dwelling (2:1-4). Born in a house, the missionary venture proceeds outward; yet it never forsakes its place of origin.[1]

Following the example of Jesus, early Christians often gathered in existing households, which not only included relatives but also slaves, freedmen, hired workers, and sometimes tenants and partners in trade or craft. Women played a dominant role in these communities because of their responsibility for the household.

The household church groups in an area

would assemble occasionally as "the whole church," and the churches of the different cities were held together by missionaries like Paul and Barnabas, by apostolic letters and finally by the written version of the Christian scriptures. The Story being told in these communities was the same story that was grasped by the first generation of disciples of Jesus and the same story that is shared in Christian communities today.

The house church was the norm in this country in the late 18th century. Places like New York City and Boston had only a few hundred Catholics and no church or resident priest. As time went on, the waves of immigrants wiped out the house churches and replaced them with edifices that rivaled each other in size, architecture and ornateness. As immigrants built their own homes, they also used their earnings to build basilica-style churches reminiscent of the churches in Europe.

The parish church, the neighborhood savings and loan association, the labor union, the precinct captain — all combined to give a neighborhood identity to urban Catholics. The Catholics in farm communities found similar devices to establish a distinctive Catholic identity. And today Hispanic Catholics, like the European immigrants before them, are struggling to shape an

American Catholic identity focused in the parish and neighborhood.

From the first American parish in New York City (St. Peter's, established in 1785), many parishes have changed their constituencies a number of times due to ethnic, racial and economic changes in the neighborhood. They are alike to the degree that they embody the North American culture and the Catholic tradition, yet they are all different because of subcultures and individual histories.

While the American parish is a unique institution in church history, it is not a community in the language of the sociologist. It is an association or a collection of individuals and communities within its geographic borders or general membership. Its contribution is that it provides an overall structure within which communities can form and it supports communities already in existence. It offers services, continuity and a larger identity. But the primary unit of church remains the small group, the "house church" modeled after those in New Testament times. A parish without satellites of hundreds of house churches in the area will be lifeless.

As the role of the parish in the community has changed, so have the expectations of its members. Parishioners are seeking a deep spiritual level of community to compensate for the spiritual void opened up in modern secular life.

Sunday liturgies are not enough. Nor are parish socials and fund raisers, the community builders in the past. The groupings today must be rooted in a conscious awareness of Jesus Christ as the center of the Christian community.

Is the Jesus Story being told and received with the excitement of the early Christians? Are house churches being born from the associations generated by the parish church? In this chapter I illustrate the answer to these questions with three parishes that have established themselves according to the house church model. Although similar to the *communidad de base* societies of Central and South America, these communities are distinctively North American.

Spirit of Peace

Ordinarily a parish is started when the bishop calls a priest and shows him a map of an area with lines drawn for the boundaries of the new parish. Masses are initially celebrated in a public school auditorium or temporary facility. A finance committee is formed and the building drive enthusiastically undertaken. After the buildings are completed, the mortgage will be the cement holding the parish together. People will come to know each other first by paying off the debt and after that, hopefully, in the breaking of the bread.

The question "Who are we as a Christian community?" is not usually part of this process. Yet this was the question posed to prospective members of Spirit of Peace in the Denver area. The parish is an experiment that makes a conscious effort to use the small community as the basic organizing principle. It tests a number of assumptions about American Catholic life. Does a parish need a resident pastor, buildings and a debt? Can a parish organize its own ministries so that the preparation for the sacraments for children, adults and new members is done by parishioners?

The formation of Spirit of Peace was the product of discussions over a period of years at national and diocesan levels. It was presented as an experiment in team ministry in anticipation of the emerging crisis of parishes without priests. Father Dan Flaherty wanted to add to the experiment. He suggested a parish without buildings and a debt. He argued that the money and energies used in fund raising could be channeled into salaries of non-clerical professional ministers.[2]

After months of shaping their views, the team settled on Longmont, a Denver suburb, that had petitioned for a second parish. An invitation was sent to Catholics in the Denver area to meet with the team and discuss the new concept of parish. Several hundred people attended out of which 30 people emerged who were interested in the parish concept. They then participated in an intensive six-week training session before the parish opened.

Spirit of Peace shares its office and worship space with a Presbyterian church in this plush Denver suburb. The full-time pastoral team includes a sister, a young layman with a degree in theology, a lay woman and a married couple. Father Flaherty comes every other Sunday and during the week for staff meetings. While he is pastor in a sense, his primary responsibility and his residence is at another long established parish. A number of other priests take turns on the alternate Sunday.

The essence of the Spirit of Peace community is in its network of base communities. Twelve groups started at the first organizing meeting. Four years later most are still in existence. Some split into smaller groups because of size, and new communities continue to form. Membership in a small group is not required for parish membership, but it is stressed.

When the parish was formed, parishioners

signed up with the group that most interested them. Several wanted family-oriented communities, including one centering on families with teen-age young people. Another community was headed by three retired couples, but they attracted people of all ages, even one junior high student who remained with the group for a year. Several communities decided on a scripture/ prayer orientation, while another chose to focus on current events. All clearly understood that each group would determine its direction. Each group is expected to name itself and draw up a covenant, signed by each member. At the end of each year, the covenant is reviewed and discussed before it is renewed.

While each community makes decisions about the content of its meetings, there is an overarching structure for all communities. A biblically based book is recommended annually as discussion material for all communities. Attendance at bible studies sponsored by local churches is encouraged. Bible readings, song, quiet time and prayers of petition are part of all meetings.

Religious education and sacramental preparation are done within the small communities. Parents decide whether or to what degree they want their entire family involved in these areas. In preparing for the various sacraments, a team

member or a parishioner meets with the parents
to begin the process. Usually the parents decide
to do the majority of the preparation in a group
and volunteer their homes. Each contributes various individual gifts in preparing the liturgy for
reception of the sacrament which is then celebrated with the entire parish gathered. The role
of the religious educator is "to discover the talents for ministry in others and then to promote
those talents."

Outreach is a given for each group. "It has
been our experience," reports Spirit of Peace parishioner Rose Mullen, "that as a community
goes beyond itself in service to others the group
becomes a much stronger community. There is
something rewarding about several families or
individuals becoming involved in the same task.
It increases their awareness." One of the team
members has encouraged communities to become involved in everything from building an
emergency shelter and remodeling a home to be
used for battered women, to helping refugee
families in Thailand.

When one joins the parish, there is an invitation, if not an expectation, to join a small community. Can this model take root in American
soil? After four years the answers to these questions are beginning to emerge. There is no in-

stant community at Spirit of Peace as there is instant coffee. A staff member said that it will take a decade for people to relate with each other at a deep level. But while this is a high tech area, with professionals only a phone call away from the moving van, parishioners still find ways to relate to each other at significant depths over a short period of time.

The glue that holds these small communities together, besides the structured meetings, liturgies, sacramental preparations and outreach projects, are the holiday potlucks, parish soup suppers and relaxed get-togethers among the families in the summer.

St. Catherine-St. Lucy

St. Catherine-St. Lucy church is on the Oak Park side of Austin Avenue, which separates Oak Park from Chicago. It is a relatively small parish with a high profile. It is on the cutting edge of RCIA, providing aid to Nicaragua and organizing base communities. The parish attracts highly articulate Catholics, who can argue both sides of an issue in the parish bulletin. Sister Teresita Wend, a pastoral associate, is an unusually gifted liturgist, homilist, RCIA coordinator and spiritual leader. Sister Mary Lunardi's skills are in spiritual direction and organizing base communities.

Sister Mary sent out a call for parishioners to join small, intentional communities based on the Latin American *communidad de base*. The call came through the parish bulletin, but also from her personal invitations. The groups now have a five-year history.

Like a family, each group develops a life and spirit of its own, but all subscribe to a basic format. They meet every two weeks in each other's homes. The central focus of the meeting is a discussion of a scripture passage or an article with a scriptural orientation. The choice is made by the host.

I was intrigued by the dynamic that held these people together. How do people who serve on civic boards and parish committees, who belong to professional organizations and are generally activists find time to come? The answer is simple. "Just block off Tuesday night. Let everyone know that you are unavailable that night." For these people, their meetings have become a priority.

The oldest member of one group I met was 80. He was a blind and feeble man from the Chicago side of the parish, whose children had deserted him. He was brought to and from the meetings by another member. The oldest members of a second group were a couple married 42 years. The group also included a newly-wed couple, newcomers to the community. In both groups there were single parents and spouses whose partners did not choose to be members. The span of occupations was equally diverse.

What keeps them coming? The answers vary. One said, "I could only belong to church on these terms. I am on the parish liturgy committee; it is not enough. Parish membership is too anonymous." The blind man said, "My children deserted me. This is a group where I experience love." A single parent told me, "I am not sure if I can accept everything the church stands for, but I like this group for the relationships. The people here are closer to me than my best friends because I see them more often. The parties and phone calls keep it alive." It was also apparent that it was scripture and the faith commitment of the group that gave strength to each and created a bonding.

The base communities are clearly a part of St. Catherine-St. Lucy parish. Sister Mary facilitates communication with the staff and a pulpit pitch at the end of Sunday liturgies is used to invite new members.

Our Lady of Guadalupe

Our Lady of Guadalupe in San Jose could be a parish in any California city where the con-

centration of Mexicans makes Spanish the language of the street and the liturgy. Franciscan
Brother Edward Dunn came to the parish staff
with experience in developing base communities
both in Latin America and in a Nevada parish.
His primary responsibilities in the parish are
communidad de base, RENEW and community organization. He is very articulate about these
three elements working together as a triad.

Two years ago a door-to-door census con-
ducted by parishioners revealed a desire to form
small groups. Ten out of the 12 groups formed at
this time remain, with anywhere from eight to 17
members in a group. Half are neighborhood
groups, people on the block or around the corner, and the other half are friends and relatives.

A 15-member committee assumes responsibility for networking, preparing programs and
training group leaders. They have adapted the
RENEW model with two intense six-week sessions in the fall and Lent. The meetings during
these series consist of scripture studies, prayers
of the faithful, a speaker and a potluck. Two of
the groups found 12 weeks insufficient and meet
every week. Most groups meet Friday or Saturday evening.

Our Lady of Guadalupe also works with
other parishes in the area who follow this model

of combining *communidad de base*, RENEW and community organization, although each parish has its own style. Once a year all the groups in the four parishes have a get-together.

Brother Dunn offers a theory for why this type of organization has worked at Our Lady of Guadalupe: "The most successful efforts to form basic community in the United States have been among the Hispanics, parishes that are 90 or 95 percent Mexican or Mexican American. There is a basic desire among them to be part of a smaller unit they can trust and where they can experience their faith at a base level. In the Mexican culture there is a desire to build relationships in the neighborhood, to share the faith at another level."

Outreach also becomes an important dimension of the small communities. "For the past 15 years our parish has been involved in issues that concern the community, going back to Cesar Chavez and the farm workers," says Brother Dunn. "Now we are saying to the base communities that these community concerns are a part of the small group. The small community provides theological reflection for our community action."

Spirit of Peace, St. Catherine-St. Lucy and Our Lady of Guadalupe offer modern versions of the house church of the first centuries. Merely imitating these models would be a mistake. Parishes need to experiment creatively with these models, according to their own unique histories. To be viable in the next century, parishes must encourage parishioners to believe in the value of "two or three gathered together" in the Lord's name.

Notes

1. John Koenig, *New Testament Hospitality*, Fortress, Philadelphia, 1985, p. 103.

2. Daniel Flaherty, "No Pastor, No Building, No Debt, Still a Parish," *Church*, Fall, 1985.

Chapter Six

No-Priest Parishes

According to researcher Robert McClory, the phenomenon of no-priest parishes "is increasing every year and although it is initially a painful experience for the parishioners affected, it is apparently producing important side effects that may well profoundly shape the church of the future."[1]

The causes of the phenomenon are celibacy and the ban on women's ordination. There is a shortage of priests, yet vocations abound among women who experience the call and men who do not have the charism of celibacy.

Since the church chooses not to close parishes even though there is no priest available, the Code of Canon Law has made provision for no-priest parishes:

> If, because of a shortage of priests, the diocesan Bishop has judged that a deacon, or

some other person who is not a priest, or a
community of persons, should be entrusted
with a share in the exercise of the pastoral
care of a parish, he is to appoint some priest
who, with the powers and faculties of a parish priest, will direct the pastoral care.[2]

Preparing men and women, other than
priests and religious, to "be entrusted with a
share in the exercise of the pastoral care of a parish" must be placed high on the agenda of diocesan and parish administrators. They must grap-
ple with increasing their allotment for training
parishioners as para-professional ministers at the
expense of other budgeted items.

A few theology schools in this country have
opened their enrollment to lay people on an
equal footing with those preparing for ordination. While this has been done primarily in
schools owned and operated by religious communities of men, it is frowned upon by the Vatican.

The change will come when dioceses encourage and recruit lay professionals, rather than
reluctantly allowing occasional lay people to take
courses.

The American Catholic church is presently a
clericalized church. There are no visible signs of
the church advocating a declericalized ministry.

Yet it is happening at the grassroots. Many national hierarchies in the Third World have accepted a laicized church, not as the only viable option available, but as an ideal which approximates the church of the New Testament.

Peter Gilmore of the Institute of Pastoral Studies at Chicago's Loyola University asserts: "There's no question that a move is beginning. It's born both out of contemporary theology as well as necessity. The Vatican II idea that the church belongs to the people, combined with the shrinking clergy population, has conspired to create a different atmosphere which will demand a rethinking of the notion of priesthood. Now parishes tend to see themselves as fully existing, legitimate communities even if no priest is attached."[3]

In spite of lack of institutional support, parishes must begin planning for no-priest parishes. We need to do more than commission people for ministry. Ministry requires skills which can be transmitted by in-service training of recruits. If we want quality parish ministry, we must provide quality training for staff and volunteers. Goodwill and the freedom to minister are not enough. Skills must be acquired, accountability demanded and a support system provided.

"I am looking forward to being a parish ad-

ministrator. I have the skills. In ten years lay people like myself will be needed." Linda DeManti is
not presently a parish administrator, but she is
one of the hundreds of lay people ready and
willing to be parish administrators in parishes
where there are no resident priests or in parishes
where the pastor wants to devote full time to being a pastor rather than an administrator. She is
half-time staff liturgist for St. Patrick's Cathedral
in San Jose and is very clear about having the
necessary skills. "I am not called to preside, but
there are priests who do not like to be administrators. I like to work on budgets.

"Since 1971 I did volunteer work in posi-
tions at a Newman center and parishes. I took
courses and workshops relating to the particular
ministries in which I was engaged. Presently I
am the liturgy director, coordinating the music
and environment that shape a prayerful liturgy.
My job involves organizing training sessions for
each of the liturgical ministries and calling forth
people to assume these ministries. For example,
communion ministers are called forth from the
community by nomination for a two-year period.
I do not work directly with RENEW but I do
meet members and draw some of them into liturgical roles.

"I have a broad background in both finances and ministry that would serve me well as a parish administrator. In the neighboring diocese of Sacramento there are four parishes without resident pastors. Two of them have lay administrators. Our diocese will be moving into no-pastor parishes. I will be ready to serve one of them as parish administrator."

A theology of empowerment is beginning to touch the fault line in our understanding of church with earthshaking potential. Sister Kristin Roth, "pastor" of two parishes in Missouri, sees a changing perception of the sacraments. "I think the people are growing in their awareness that often the reality of a sacramental occurrence does not necessarily take place when the ritual is celebrated. When we celebrate the sacrament of baptism, the priest pours the water but I'm standing up there next to him. When we walk out of the church, I hold the baby in my hands and say, 'This is the newest member of our parish family.' The people have commented that this seemed right."

Sister Kristin's experience opens a Pandora's Box for seminary professors preparing young men for the traditional form of parish ministry in which the identity of the priest has been centered around his saying the correct ritual words that transform the human into the divine. When

the sacramental grace is experienced as flowing
from the entire rite celebrated in a vibrant faith
community rather than the mechanical perfec-
tion of his words and actions, we will have a sacramental revolution in the pews or wherever
God's grace is mediated in the name of the
church.

According to Gilmore, the pastoral administrator experience tends to bring into focus two
distinct theologies about sacraments.

> The more traditional approach stresses the
> *magic moment* when grace is conferred, pro-
> vided the matter and form of the sacrament
> are present. Whether the sacramental minis-
> ter has prepared the person for the reception
> or even known them is largely irrelevant.
> Contemporary theology, on the other hand,
> stresses the *process* by which a person comes
> to the sacramental reception, so that in the
> baptism of an adult, for example, the salvific
> faith commitment occurs long before the wa-
> ter is poured. In a normal parish where a
> priest is involved at least to some extent in
> the process, the two theologies do not clash.
> In a priestless parish, where the sacramental
> process and preparation are conducted by a
> non-ordained person, people begin to won-
> der why a virtually unknown "holy man"
> must be called in to function at the climactic
> moment and then disappear — wheth-

er the occasion be a Sunday liturgy, a baptism, confession or marriage.[4]

Sister Kristin describes a visit to an ailing 65-year-old man in a local hospital. "He drew me down to where he was lying in the bed and said, 'Bless me, Father, for I have sinned.' And he told me all the things he would have talked to the priest about. I wasn't sure what I was going to do so I just laid my hands on him and I asked the Lord to hear his prayer and forgive him his sins. I did not say 'I absolve you in the name of the Father, Son and Holy Spirit.' At the end I said, 'What do you think happened here?' and he said, 'God forgave me my sins.' I told him that technically this was not what we call sacramental confession, that I didn't have the power to forgive his sins, as it were, legally. And he said, 'It doesn't make any difference to me whether it's you or Father Hoffman. I got it out of my heart and talked to the Lord about it, right?' "

Albion, Indiana

Sister Jo-Ann Brdecka had a Master of Divinity and several years of experience as a pastoral minister of the 109-year-old Blessed Sacrament church in Albion, Indiana. The Ministry Agreement under which she held this position read:

Under the authority and directive of the diocesan Bishop, the pastoral associate will assume responsibility for the pastoral care of
the parish. Except for that ministry which
calls specifically for a priest signed with or-
ders, the pastoral associate is bound by obligation to see to it that the word of God in its
integrity is announced to those living in the
parish. She shall see to it that the goods of
the parish are properly administrated and
that the baptismal, marriage and death regis-
ters are accurately inscribed and carefully
preserved. In all matters of parish life she
should cooperate with the bishop and with
the presbyterate of the diocese.[5]

Blessed Sacrament had always been served
by visiting priests. Until her death after a long ill-
ness in August of 1986, Sister Jo-Ann lived in the
rectory and offered all the pastoral services that
do not require an ordained priest. A retired
priest living in the area presided at the Sunday
liturgy. The registered families increased from 80
to 105 in the three years since Sister Jo-Ann arrived. "My initial visible leadership," reported
Sister Jo-Ann, "was encouraging to people, as-
sisting them in seeing their council and committee roles, helping them develop agendas and organization. My role continues to be one of
fine-tuning the now functioning leaders to grow
in confidence, experience and depth."[6]

Flint, Michigan

When the pastor of Sacred Heart parish in Flint, Michigan was transferred in 1984, Bishop Kenneth Povish informed the parishioners that he had no priest to assign them. The parish of 600 registered parishioners, of which 300 were active, petitioned the bishop through its leadership to appoint Patricia Robertson-Berger and Kenneth Berger, husband and wife, to be pastoral administrators.

Pat had pastoral experience in campus ministry. Ken had studied for the priesthood with a religious order and left nine months before ordination. They met while working in an overnight shelter for the homeless and spent the early years of their married life working with migrant farmworkers, and helping in soup kitchens. They had also been jailed for non-violent acts of civil disobedience. When they heard of the opening in Flint they said, "Why not?" They had talked about doing this at some stage of their life.

"As pastoral administrators we do everything a priest does except for those things one must be ordained to do. Ninety percent of our ministry is pastoral and ten percent is business management — lights, leaks, locks, leases. It can confuse the people in the benches who see

administrators as head bookkeepers. To avoid
confusion we refer to ourselves as pastoral ministers. Some priests in the area refer to us as the
pastors of Sacred Heart."

Sacred Heart has one liturgy each weekend.
Priests from the area and around the diocese
who are available come in to preside. Having different celebrants gives the liturgy a variety of
styles. The Bergers say it also enables the people
to relate to them as pastors rather than as the
Sunday presider. Canon 766 and its warrant for
lay preaching allows one of them to preach at
least one Sunday each month. "We see this as
crucial since there are times when it is important
for resident pastoral ministers rather than a visitor to apply the message of the scriptures to their
community."

Breaking ground in this way hasn't been
without its disadvantages for the Bergers. "We
came to the ministry of pastoring without the
usual three or more years under a seasoned pastor like most priests have before they become
pastors. While we missed that training, we have
received a good deal of behind the scenes help
and advice from other Catholic pastors, particularly our canonical pastor.

"There are times when it seems that it
would be easier for all concerned if we were an

ordained male and not an unordained couple with a baby. We would be deceiving ourselves if we said all the people are perfectly content with the present situation. We would also be deceiving ourselves if we thought we would be as warmly accepted in other parishes as we have been in Sacred Heart."

Yet it would seem that this experiment in ministry is working. The fact that priestless parishes are thriving, growing communities, brings to the fore another point for reflection. Does an ordained person necessarily make the best pastor of a given community? Or should the pastoring be left to those who have that particular charism? Present legislation does not allow an entire category of gifted pastors to be ordained in the Roman rite.

Hillsdale, Michigan

Hillsdale is the county seat for a farm area in lower Michigan. Broad Street is a busy shopping and commercial center for farm families. St. Anthony's church sits opposite the government building and the adjacent park, next to the Episcopal church. In the rear is the religious education building, the former Catholic school, which closed in 1985. The parish serves 600 Catholics who make up 4 percent of the population in the 30-by-30 mile county.

The pastor, Father Timothy Crowley, a young man in his thirties, and a former student of mine, was not home when I arrived one rainy morning in April. I had an opportunity to talk with Sister Maryetta Churches, the director of religious education, and James Corder, the youth minister. They are the full-time pastoral team assembled by Father Tim two years ago.

Sister Maryetta has 250 enrolled in the growing religious education program. She has many other ministerial roles including spiritual director to ten parishioners, mostly women in their 30s and 40s. She is available to all parishioners and is very knowledgeable about their family concerns and the government agencies which offer services, particularly for women.

Jim Corder, the youth minister of eight months, is 22 and planning to marry soon. The youth minister in his home parish in Flint, with whom he worked, challenged him to consider the call to youth ministry. This is the language a priest vocation director would use in encouraging a generous, energetic, creative and faith-filled young man to enter the seminary. Jim went to Orchard Lake Seminary in Detroit for a year for the theological underpinning he needed for a career as youth minister.

Jim's goals are very clear. He sees Father

Tim as a young priest whose skills and success are so obvious that the bishop will move him to a parish with greater responsibility, or he will simply move as all pastors do in the era of limited tenure. The next pastor, Jim tells me, may not be interested in youth ministry and might eliminate the position. Therefore, Jim has a time frame in which to develop a parish youth ministry that will be self-sustaining after both he and Father Tim move on.

The parish is moving toward a community model, rather than the old model where people came to Mass on Sunday, sat in *their* pews, dutifully worshiped, and returned to their town or farm homes without knowing each other. Now people come to know and share their lives and their faith in many interlocking relationships.

Could St. Anthony's be a no-resident priest parish in a decade? Getting a resident priest pastor will be increasingly difficult in rural areas. The concentration of supply, or weekend priests, is in large cities that have huge Catholic institutions with priest teachers and administrators. The diocesan circuit-rider priest doing liturgies for several parishes on a rotation basis may not be an attractive vocation for a priest who feels called to share his life with people whom he relates to as a shepherd and can share their joys and sorrows on a daily basis. The situation may call for a circuit rider who is a theologian, not necessarily a priest, who is at the service of pastoral administrators rather than available to an entire flock or even several flocks.

Notes

1. Robert McClory, "Priestless Parishes Burgeon," *National Catholic Reporter*, August 29, 1986, p. 11.

2. *Code of Canon Law,* canon 766.

3. McClory, "Priestless Parishes Burgeon," p. 30.

4. Ibid.

5. UPTURN, February/March, 1985, p. 6.

6. Ibid.

Chapter Seven

A Communitarian Spirituality

Every significant impact which Christianity has made upon the social order in modern times has been built upon the pious lay conventicle, the small group of pious transformation, the small church within the Church, which strenuously combines religious socialization and the deepening in Christian self-identity with a steadfast insistence on worldly service and action.

Max Weber

In this book we have focused on the parish as the ordinary North American way of shaping community — the twos and threes coming together in the name of the Lord to share their journeys. The parish renewal programs, the liturgical and peace and justice commissions, community organization projects, shelters and food pantries are the places where people work together and find spiritual companions.

The parish has been only one form of community in the history of the church. While it has served the majority, other Christians have felt called to a radical community lifestyle as they pursue radical interpretations of the gospel. It is these intense, single-purposed, countercultural groups that ultimately shape Christianity and influence the parishes with which they were never really affiliated.

In every century groups of Christians emerge who want to live an intense Christian life with a specific focus. They create their own form of community, which the church may or may not accept at a later date. A vital Christianity cannot be locked into a single form. Religious life evolved from hermits who wanted to escape the world. St. Benedict, St. Francis, St. Clare, and others shaped forms to fit monks, cloistered sisters, and itinerant preachers. St. Ignatius founded a militaristic core of men serving the pope.

While young people today may have this same intense desire to serve the poor or oppressed within a framework of community living, the permanent commitment of the traditional religious life is not as attractive as it had been earlier in this century. The dedicated young men and women who in the past would have

entered our novitiates and seminaries now gravi-
tate toward volunteer programs, where they can
test their wings in a community life setting for a
limited number of years. Maryknoll Volunteers
has a waiting list too long for most applicants to
wait.

A few people are graced to go down into
the well of themselves and touch the under-
ground stream, experiencing the transcendent
God in a way that has changed their lives. It is
the story of Jacob wrestling with God disguised
as an angel and being marked for life. The vision
of what they are called to be is overpowering and
cannot be undertaken alone. They need a supporting community as did Jesus.

One of the most celebrated American communities — not a parish or a religious order —
is The Catholic Worker. It has a highly focused
and radical gospel agenda which a traditional
parish could not abide. While the Catholic
Worker is Catholic in orientation, it has never
questioned people who join about their religious
affiliation. Many of their most significant members, such as pacifist Emman Hennacy, have had
no religious background, nor did they all ultimately become Catholics. The Catholic Worker
believed passionately in individual freedom. It
was likewise free from the structure of church

authority, which allowed it to criticize the Catholic church, essentially pledging loyalty to the church with immunity.

The sanctuary movement and less ideological forms of caring such as soup kitchens and shelters for the homeless are bringing about a variety of ecumenical communities. The emphasis is on the task rather than the content of religious traditions and doctrines. This is not radically different from the long traditions of religious communities, for there too the task determined the community. Since the world as they experienced it was Catholic, it was only natural that the communities would also be Catholic.

In a society where religion, like so much else, is pluralistic, we can expect that communities that come together will be ecumenical, leaving room for people to find ways to worship in churches within their chosen tradition, while attending to the task of living a commitment to justice and compassion.

In two visits to San Jose — separated by two years — I met with Peggy Coleman. In both interviews the subjects were Loaves and Fishes, a community meal program for the poor, and her spiritual life. With Peggy they are integral. One cannot exist without the other.

Loaves and Fishes has a large staff, about

35, with co-directors as well as a board of directors, two janitors, two language teachers, two cooks. Besides the kitchen and dining room it also has a clothing room. Peggy explains, "We employ the people we serve. We want to give people jobs, a way of helping them get out." Loaves and Fishes also rents a home for people in transition. Presently it has men and women and a little girl.

"Last night we had a party for the new co-director for our Loaves and Fishes team. In working on developing the team for five or six years, we have become a community. We receive nurture from each other as we come to know each other 'in the breaking of the bread.'

"If you are really into working with the poor, it energizes you. It is not like sitting at a desk. Look what happened to St. Francis when he kissed the leper. I understand why Christ liked to be with the poor. In studying his life you can see that he had friends from every status. All were important, but he seemed most comfortable with the poor. It is life-giving, energizing. You have no expectations of people. You can really be who you are. People come here and no one asks their history or how much money they have in their pocket. There is no competition, no trying to be somebody, no categories, no expectations, no judgments. There is no status here. It doesn't matter if you are a street person who has come in for a meal, or if you are an executive who has come in to serve."

Conversion is an important aspect of Peggy Coleman's spirituality. She says, "The conversion I see is becoming more compassionate, not coming in with an agenda but allowing life to come together."

Peggy has strong ties to the Catholic tradition, which give her roots from which her dedication to serving grows. She grew up in a poor section of Santa Monica, near Venice Beach and saw a lot of poverty. "I went to a Catholic school and heard stories of mothers who were prostitutes and lived in cars. Often I had to walk through alcoholics to get to school."

She expresses a deep love for the church. "I grew up in an era when everything revolved around the parish. My parents were very involved in the church. It was a great support for us. It was our community. In my Irish Catholic home, church, school and family were tightly knit in a secure life. My father was a milkman with five children, but we always had what we needed. I have good memories of the church. I was one step away from becoming a sister when I decided to marry."

Perhaps because of this background, Peggy is committed to community life. She and her husband belong to a Franciscan community that also includes a Franciscan brother, another couple and a probation officer. There are also four families who are members of the community but maintain their own residences. A few of them meet two mornings a week for morning prayers, and the entire community meets every other Saturday for a meeting, dinner and a non-eucharistic prayer service.

"The exodus is not our biblical image as it is with the Catholic Worker, which means leaving the whole American thing behind, a radical separation from American values. We are spiritual people who want to keep our spirituality alive but not through the desert image of fleeing. We are searching to keep God alive in our lives. We go to different parishes. We are not trying to create a whole new church, but simply to live gospel values through supporting one another, trying to live in a very complex society and maintain our spiritual roots. I cannot live in the inner city without community. Our biblical metaphor is Jesus walking with his disciples, living with them. If Christ came as a guru and never formed a community, he would not last. He came to form community."

The Peggy Colemans will always be the remnant of Israel, the sign of the kingdom. To come in close contact with a person like her and to let yourself be changed by the presence is to permit the Christianity of the first century to happen in our lives.

This is not to put one type of holiness above another. Many people heroically struggle to get out of bed in the morning and face a world in which the best they can do is cope. They are one of a variety of saints among us. Each is gifted by the same Spirit. Christianity is alive and well in both our heroes and our survivors.

Christ House in the Adams Morgan district of Washington, D.C., is a model Christian community of people in the medical profession. Two doctors and their families, two religious women and a number of full-time volunteers live and work with the homeless sick. Each Sunday they come together to share a meal, to give an accounting of their spiritual lives for the week, to share in a scriptural service and to conduct house business.

"All of us decide," explained Sister Marcella Jordon, "to reflect on what spiritual means we need to nourish ourselves. As Catholic sisters, we feel daily Mass and evening examen is important. We name these things to the group and are accountable for them each week when we meet."[1]

The Protestant churches across the country have spawned a number of small communities outside of traditional parish structures. The evangelicals have given us Sojourners in Washington, D.C., a lay community that has developed a community of peacemakers within the evangelical tradition. Through their monthly magazine *Sojourners* they have had an impact on the Catholic peace communities across the country. Sojourners in turn have been enriched by their appreciation of the Catholic tradition of community and the spirituality that grew out of it. There has been a dynamic interchange between Jim Wallis, the Sojourners leader, and Father Richard Rohr, the founder of the New Jerusalem Community in Cincinnati. Jim Wallis offered the New Jerusalem Community a highly developed intellectual, radical activist peace agenda. Richard Rohr offered to Sojourners the Franciscan tradition of poverty and community.

The Church of Our Saviour in Washington, D.C., is not a typical parish that brings the total community together for worship. The focus is on small communities of people who choose a particular marketplace ministry that is tied into their work life. A highly specialized ministry and an

intense community life are the equally posi-
tioned facets of community.

Gordon Cosby is the founder and pastor of
the Church of Our Saviour. Commitment to the
community must continue to grow and intensify.
"It seems to me that individualism is so strong in
each of us that we have to be converted step by
step to get to the place where we really are corporate people. Becoming a corporate person has
to happen step by step because community is
very, very frightening and extremely difficult.
Community is hell for many, many people.

"I think the average person who comes into
a Christian community wants support for his or
her life, but feels that they must make funda-
mental decisions themselves. They want to be associated with a group of people that is doing significant things and is on the right side of the
issues. But they are not at all ready to surrender
any part of their sovereignty to a larger call."[2]

Such "parishes" exist in every large metropolitan area. It may be a tiny Mennonite church
in a suburb or a Wellington Street Congrega-
tional Church in a densely populated Yuppie
area of Chicago. Unlike Catholic parishes, they
are covenanted communities. Members enter as
novices to experience the life of the community.
It may demand special classes and weekends of

commitment, as does St. Mark's Episcopal church in the shadow of the nation's capitol. After the probationary period the community discerns with the prospective members whether this community is what they seek and whether they are willing to enter a covenant. Many parishes like St. Mark's accept dual membership. Even if one does not join the covenanted community, one is still welcome to worship on Sunday. The intensity of community life and accountability for one's work and leisure aspects of life will vary, but the distinguishing characteristic is the biblical notion of covenant.

The road to Jerusalem is filled with disappointments and frustrations. The Jesus Story cannot live outside of a community. The members of the community support each other in their countercultural style of living. They do not reject their denominational heritage, but rather treasure it for the connections and continuity it offers them without being constrained by its institutional structures.

It must be the concern of all Christians who have been touched by the Jesus Story to widen the circle of community, to bring the lonely, the hurting, the survivors into relationship with others at whatever level possible. The Story rooted in a community is a lifeline for the people who

fall between the cracks in our individualistic society.

Notes

1. Arthur Jones, *National Catholic Reporter*, June
20, 1986, p. 1.

2. Gordon Cosby, "The Call to Community," *Sojourners*, July 1986, p. 17.

Summing Up:

The North American Parish Story

Innovative parishes that focus on the development of small communities as an organizing principle have been featured in this book as the parishes of the future. They are among the thousands of parishes across the country that have accepted the challenge to put their energies into a new kind of church. They challenge the post-immigrant sacramental or consumer parish to re-interpret its past and move toward new images of church.

Yet, we need to face the stark reality of the enduring presence and power of the sacramental parish. Concentrated in large metropolitan areas such as Boston, New York, Philadelphia, Chicago, and Los Angeles, where there is no shortage of priests on weekends, they have traditionally been the source of change in the American Catholic church.

Parishioners in the consumer parish may want good homilies, good music, and celebrations that flow, but these things are mere commodities offered by the parish staff.

This observation is not an indictment of the depth of religious conviction, depth of contemplative prayer, or sense of Mass as sacred mystery among such churchgoers. It speaks to an individualistic or consumer approach to liturgy. The consumer approach applies also to people who parish hop for good liturgies without volunteering to be lectors, greeters, eucharistic ministers, or servers at the community meal. These people miss the demand that the gospel makes on all Christians to serve their community.

Nor is this negative view a reflection on traditional parish leadership. It is a statement about the sacramental parish — once the backbone of the American Catholic church — now being caught in an ideological transition that debilitates the efforts of staff to lead the parishes into the refreshing waters of a community structure.

Nor does it mean that the liturgical reforms of Vatican II have not been implemented according to the diocesan directives. Rare is the parish that does not have lay lectors and eucharistic ministers at weekend liturgies. However, participation in our liturgies points up the gap between what we hold as renewed Catholics and our performance which is embedded in us from our individualist culture.

My concern and goal in writing this book have been to show the renewal of the sacramental parish, to profile some that are moving into the mainstream of life. They help demonstrate how we can reconnect the sacramental signs to life on the street, in the home, and at work; how we can close the gap between the church ritual and the earthiness of life; how we can reshape parish life to sense that we are celebrating the presence of the risen Christ in our midst.

How can we encourage all parishes to center on relationships that bring the sacraments to life, celebrating the grace of God rather than merely performing lifeless, perfunctory rituals? Sacraments are experienced as life-giving when there is a community, not merely a crowd of individuals doing the same thing at the same time. The sacraments were given to us to bring the Story to life through our ordinary experiences.

In the new vision of parish life, unstructured small groups stimulate people to experience the Emmaus event of finding Jesus in the breaking of the bread, in applying the message of the scriptures to daily life, in giving hospitality to the stranger.

If the parish is to attract people to the gospel message and present the Story as a challenge to modern life, the triad of liturgy, formation, and outreach through prophetic utterance and deed must be present. In every parish story presented in this book, liturgy is an integral part of the formation process and the liturgy is enlivened by people who emerge from the initiation rites. But without a strong outreach, liturgy and formation limp.

Liturgy

Liturgy tends to be paralyzed by rigid parish structures that haven't adapted to contemporary life. People over 40 are inclined to hold on to precious memories from their youth, but in the process deny to their children the opportunity to reshape the liturgy and express their own religious experience. Liturgy may simply have to die to be born again from the life experiences and cultural demands of younger people. Parishes need to be converted and live or become museum pieces supported only by precious memories.

The Catholic church of the First World, in contrast to the church of the Third World, may be too embedded in time-bound structures that express the profound religious values of previous generations but have little meaning today. The church of Zaire in central Africa presents a contrast.

> The story of the people of Zaire remains unfinished; it is still being lived. Their church is unique. From heavy institutionalized structures imported from the West it has changed to become a church of vital and vibrant communities. From pyramid structures it has changed to become lay-centered — with both women and men holding leadership roles. From worship centered, it has changed to become life centered.
>
> It is this Eucharist, this life that is lived in the streets and neighborhoods, that is ritualized and celebrated in liturgy, using traditional African symbols, dance expressions and literary genre. Despite intense and continual suffering the people of Zaire always celebrate life.[1]

We cannot impose the African model on the North American experience, any more than we can copy the *communidad de base*. This would be as much of a cultural violation as the missionaries who imposed the standards of 19th-century Western Europe on its colonies or expecting the Third World societies of today to copy our corporate, committee-oriented structures.

We are always searching for the inner dy-

namic that is common to the human spirit and
the Christian tradition so that we can express our
creative experiences in our own cultural context.
The lesson we learn from Zaire is the need to
break through our American parish structures
while preserving the core of the tradition that is
common to the Catholic experience of the structures of other cultures and centuries. Liturgy
and other parochial structures must become po-
rous enough to allow the Spirit life of our street,
home and work place to surface.

Liturgy must pull together the experience of
Christian living that is present in the community's expression of life. Today's most creative liturgies seem to take place among people struggling to become community rather than among a
coincidental collection of parishioners who registered in the nearest Catholic church. The
greeters, the music and the well-prepared homilies make good liturgies wellsprings for life because they draw on the well of the community itself for their spiritual strength.

St. Clement's insists that liturgy is not the
totality of Christian life. Its liturgies are soul fill-
ing. Sacred Heart, the no-priest Flint parish, has
warm liturgical celebrations because the relationships among the people exude warmth. Blessed
Sacrament in West Virginia has liturgies where

one feels the Lord's presence in the air one breathes.

Formation

Formation is a familiar word in the modern parish lexicon. While we associate it with the formal process of being inducted into the church or continuing a deepening process of spiritual growth, the concept is as old as the most primitive societies that had rituals of initiation and rites of passage. Because genuinely alive parishes are countercultural, they must take seriously their responsibility to help those with no introduction into the modern church to hear the Story in a community context.

The parish must utilize the method of formation that fits its history and needs. Although RCIA is the most prominent model for formation and the one approved by the institutional church, it is only a model. Each parish must take the model and make it its own if formation is going to be a vital part of renewed parish life.

St. Clare's, an older, traditional parish, uses RCIA effectively, subtly catechizing the catechists. Our Lady Gate of Heaven ties RCIA to the evangelization work through the parish school. St. Clement's finds that involving hundreds of parishioners in planning and executing liturgies achieves the formation goals of RCIA. Through *Christ Renews His Parish*, Christ the King focuses its enormous energies on bringing two new groups of parishioners each year into the depths of spiritual life and Christian witness.

Outreach

"What you do for the least of my brothers and sisters, you do for me," says Jesus. To those who respond negatively he says, "Depart from me, you cursed ones." He offers no middle ground. The injunction of Jesus is not simply laid on individuals but on every corporate enterprise.

Every parish or group that calls itself Christian must be judged by how it comes to terms with chapter 25 of Matthew's gospel. An outreach with a world view that challenges its membership is the salt that gives the parish savor. Without it the parish loses its meaning.

The parishes profiled in this book were evaluated on how well they preached and lived the prophetic dimension of the Story. Guadalupe, a Mexican parish in San Jose, publicly proclaims its dedication to a better way of living for the entire Mexican American community through community organization. St. Teresa's is a beacon calling not only parishioners and residents on Goat Hill, but the entire city of San Francisco to look at its response to political refugees. Corpus Christi, the inner-city Rochester parish, calls all suburbanites to join its community outreach to those on the margins of society. The parish calls its members to look at the systems that perpetuate the sharp and growing division between the rich and the poor. The parishioners of St. Monica's, who work in San Francisco's financial district, are challenged to examine the systems that make or break Third World countries. The pastor, Father Brian Joyce, preaches to international decision-makers the Story of a world without war and an economy that provides for all. St. Clare, St. Clement and Blessed Sacrament invite peace groups, Amnesty International, and local care groups to tell their story and appeal for volunteers.

I have tried to be sensitive to the parish staff that must mediate the wide diversity of life-styles, the range of belief of what constitutes being a Christian, and the variety of backgrounds from which the parishioners have emerged. While the leadership in the parish must take forthright stands in telling the Story, the staff cannot separate itself from the community by moving beyond its present capacity. This calls for pastoral genius. The fault too often lies on the side of timidity and a failure to trust the Spirit alive in the community.

The first-century Christians found strength in this Spirit to become a missionary church with one goal — to tell the Story, to spread the Good News about a life that has a future, a life that death changes but does not take away. When Christians met they repeated the Story the way they had heard it. They excitedly told of the acceptances and rejections they faced from people who had not been introduced to the Jesus Story. The Story was the bond that held them together, but the bond would have ceased to hold without the cause that originally brought them together, namely, the spreading of the Good News.

The Story is carried in vessels of clay and from time to time these vessels need to be broken and recast. I have tried to lay out the elements of a renewed church through a renewed parish life as a way of making vessels that can carry the Story into the future. Long live the Story!

Notes

1. *Set My People Free: Liberation Theology in Practice*, Quixote Center, Hyattsville, MD, p. 7.